'This is an extremely i resting meaning... That dou meani structure, and b ~   ionally engaging.' STUART ' LY

'A gripping read that will touch your heart...an enthralling tale beautifully written. All the ingredients for a good read are there: sadness, humour, revelations of life in a far country, but the outstanding ingredient is love. It shines from every page in this superb book; filial love, paternal love, family love. It may be moving but it is also uplifting. Read it, it will remain with you for a very long time.' SHEILA GRANT, *NewBooks Magazine*

'Uuganaa's book provides thought-provoking insight into her childhood and how cultural differences can affect the understanding and acceptance of disability. Her descriptions of the emotions are honest, heart-wrenching and reflective of those of many families. I couldn't put the book down, but I needed the tissues!' PENNY GREEN, DIRECTOR, DOWN'S HEART GROUP

'An interesting narrative of considerable cultural insight and cross-cultural value which deserves a wider readership.' COLIN NICHOLSON

'A loving testament to [a] little boy ... a beautifully constructed book, written with a refreshing directness and honesty ... a story of hope, of common humanity, of kindness and the possibility of change.' CATHERINE CZERKAWSKA

Mongol is Uuganaa Ramsay's first book. It won the Janetta Bowie Chalice Non-Fiction Book Award from the Scottish Association of Writers.

C 03 0253366

MONGOL

Uuganaa Ramsay

Saraband

Published by Saraband
Suite 202, 98 Woodlands Road
Glasgow, G3 6HB, Scotland
www.saraband.net

ISBN: 9781908643414
ebook: 9781908643421

Printed in the EU on sustainably sourced paper.

Text design by Jo Morley

3   5   7   9   10   8   6   4

The cover photograph is reproduced courtesy of the author.

www.mong___memoir.com

Author's no___
This book is ___ on ___memories. Some names have ___ changed.

Uuganaa Ramsay was born in Mongolia and grew up living in a yurt, eating marmot meat and distilling vodka from yoghurt. After winning a place on a teacher-training course she came to the UK; she now lives in Scotland with her family. Uuganaa was the Mongolian Creative Woman of the Year for Mongolians in Europe in 2012.

Author photo by Neil Thomas Douglas

Төрсөн биеийг минь заяасан
Төөрөх бүрд минь зассан
Хайраараа угжсан ижийдээ
Харцаараа бүүвэйлсэн аавдаа энэхүү номоо өргөн барья.

To Billy Buuz, our baby boy with Celtic red hair and Mongolian blue spots, who changed Mummy for the better and into a stronger person.

To U, D and S. I love you all dearly. I hope this book will let you enter Mummy's world and learn where you come from.

To my husband, whom I adore and love.

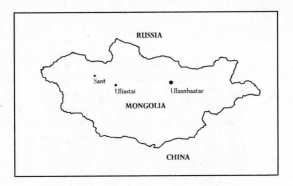

Mongolian locations in this book

CONTENTS

ONE

Billy

We don't see things as they are,
we see them as we are.

Anaïs Nin

'KISS ME AGAIN,' I said to my father, who was about to go through the Departure gate at Glasgow Airport. 'Why aren't you kissing me on my forehead like you used to?' I was looking for the comfort his kisses had been bringing me ever since I was a child. But he had thought the loose and awkward hug he'd given me earlier was 'what you do here'.

It was only March and already it was the second time he'd left Scotland this year. The middle of March in Glasgow is still winter – dark, wet and windy. We were both desperately trying hard not to sob. It is considered bad luck to cry when you say goodbye in Mongolia. I can hold on to my emotions when I say my goodbyes, even if it is to my parents, my sister or my husband. This time it was different. I was fragile and feeling vulnerable, ready to shed tears in gallons. I knew my dad was feeling the same when he quickly kissed my forehead then turned away before our tears started rolling down. As he walked away I saw him drying his eyes before turning round for a final wave.

Three months earlier, after Billy had been born, I had said to Dad over the phone, 'You have to come here. I will never forgive you if you don't.' So he had dropped everything and come from the other side of the world, from one of the remotest places on Earth – Outer Mongolia, the country where I had been raised and had lived for the first twenty-odd years of my life. My sister told me later that he had said, 'My girl doesn't cry that easily, but she sobbed on the phone. I need to go.'

At that point I'd been on my own in a room at the maternity hospital. I had asked for a single room while they were deciding where to move me from the Labour ward. I couldn't bear to look at other happy mums with their newborns, showing off their 'perfect' babies.

When I had gone routinely to see the midwife on Friday 13th November, I had been checked by a student who suggested the baby was in a breech position. Lynne, the midwife, had looked surprised and had checked my bump herself. 'Yes, it is a breech. As soon as you feel any contractions, phone the hospital immediately and go there.' The baby was due two weeks later and I didn't really think it was a big issue, knowing that I had been breech myself at birth, stuck with one leg out and giving my mum a hard time. That was in rural Mongolia in the 1970s. Now, here in Britain in 2009, I obviously had nothing to fear. They have all that they need – medical equipment and experts in this field. This should be routine, I thought.

Later that night, after having a Chinese takeaway, the contractions started to come. My husband Richard picked up the car key. 'Come on, we'll go to the hospital. You give them a call; I'll get the car ready.' We rushed to the maternity hospital leaving our other children Sara and Simon with my mum, who had arrived on her own from Mongolia just the week before. My mum was holding some milk in a bowl; she drizzled some of it on the car wheels and sprinkled some in the air after wishing us all the best, and hoping all would go well. That was her way, the Mongolian way, of wishing you the best for the future. My dear little mum in her green *deel* (the traditional Mongolian tunic, similar in length to a coat), looking worried, was trying not to offend anyone in a strange new culture, making an awful lot of effort to learn English, feeling vulnerable and powerless. Yet she is a smart, educated woman who works in a secondary school in Uliastai, a small rural town in the western part of Mongolia.

After waiting for eight hours, at about 2am the next morning it was my turn to have a C-section. I was excited; the operation was going to be nothing compared to seeing my baby. Oh, the sensation was so good when the spinal anaesthetic kicked in. Pain-free, I was ready to see my baby with my husband beside me holding my hand, both of us excited, although I could tell that he was worried, seeing me on an operating table surrounded by surgeons, nurses and an anaesthetist.

Soon after that, Billy was born, my tiny little boy, 2.5 kilos, a kilo smaller than his brother and sister had been at birth. The doctors started to check Billy immediately just like any other baby. Richard tried to look at him from where he was sitting and gasped, 'He is blonde!' with disbelief. 'Does he have the Mongolian blue spots?' I smiled. Mongolians are proud of this birthmark. Usually these blue spots appear on Asian babies when they are born and then disappear after a few months. They were still stitching me up. I then noticed a worried look on Richard's face. They seemed to be just too busy checking if Billy was all right. Then they decided to take him to the Neonatal unit. I asked, 'Please, can I see my baby before he goes?' They showed him to me from a distance as if they were hiding something and rushed him out of the room. We were worried. What's going on? Why are they not saying anything? I had a shaky feeling inside, thinking: he has abnormally big eyes; normally the vertical skin folds between the upper eyelids and inner corner of the eyes appear later in our kids.

After two, or maybe three, hours of agonised waiting and asking any passing nurse what was happening, finally a doctor and a nurse came to talk to us. I was preparing myself for the worst, scared to hear why it was and what it was that was taking them so long to come and talk to us. I heard the doctor saying, 'There are some signs of … syndrome in your baby.' I missed the main name of the syndrome. Richard was sitting beside me and I noticed his head going down between his hands, reaching his knees before he fell silent. I was trying to understand exactly what it meant, trying to know what the syndrome was.

I still had no feeling below my waist. I was high up on a bed, confused about the situation, alarmed and feeling annoyed. When I discovered they had mentioned symptoms of Down's syndrome, hundreds of questions raced through my mind: 'How long do they live?' 'What does it mean?' The doctor and the nurse were looking at us with 'poor you' eyes and the doctor's hand was on Richard's knee trying to comfort him. They said, 'Nothing is definite yet, we are just keeping you informed of the situation.' We felt angry with them for bringing that news; we could not believe our ears.

Later we went to see our Billy in the Neonatal unit. He was in an incubator, and looked so tiny and wrinkly, just like any other baby. He looked like his brother, Simon, immediately after he had been born; only, Billy had ginger hair and Simon had black hair. They both had the Mongolian blue spots on their bottoms. Billy also had a feeding tube in his mouth, which looked uncomfortable.

Richard and I were feeling anxious. The hospital had a bedside internet service for patients, and I was fervently reading about Down's syndrome, searching online to find out what it meant to have a child with a disability and how that would impact on everything. I knew very little about Down's syndrome. I had no idea that it affects the person in many different ways. The more I found out, the more I could not believe it was happening to us. I did not want it for anyone. There are things that you can change in life, like money problems and unemployment. But there was no escape in this situation. We had to accept it and get on with things. I felt like shaking my body to get rid of this hurt from myself and my family. There was nothing to do but accept it and deal with it. It wasn't easy to come to terms with the situation though.

It was hard for Richard too. I had a room for myself to cry, and the nurses and midwives were very supportive, whereas he had to go home and behave as if everything was fine. My mum especially would be waiting for him to come from the hospital and be excited about the arrival of our new baby. Richard could not speak Mongolian. So it was harder in some ways and easier in others. He couldn't properly explain what was happening to my mum. Although Sara could speak both languages, we didn't want to upset the kids until we were more certain about Billy's diagnosis. The only person Richard could have confided in was his own mum. But she was now in a geriatric hospital, waiting to be transferred to a nursing home.

Later that day, Richard brought the kids and my mum to see me and Billy. It was so good to see Sara and Simon. I was feeling very down and had red, swollen eyes because of crying so much. I tried to look happy and upbeat for my kids and my mum. I had Billy's photo with me. So the kids saw their baby brother's photo before they saw Billy. They were so excited and went to see him in the Neonatal unit. When they came back they were asking when Billy and I were coming home. I said we would know in a few days' time.

Richard had scanned Billy's photo and put it on a newly built website in Billy's Mongolian name – Dorj. It was for my friends and relatives in Mongolia. If I were in Mongolia, my uncles and aunts would all have come to see us. I was glad that I wasn't in Mongolia at this time. I couldn't face seeing people and pretending everything was fine. I had wished I was in Mongolia when Simon was born. I remember all the other mums had flowers, cards and balloons beside their beds. Simon and I had a card that Sara had made from a magazine saying 'Get well' until Richard brought me a beautiful bouquet of flowers.

The next day was Sunday. We spoke to the consultant in charge and had a glimpse of good news. 'I'm sorry for causing stress and concern yesterday. I don't think your baby has Down's syndrome. Perhaps we were confused with your background and physical features.' What a relief. We suddenly felt so much better, everything seemed brighter and we could breathe. The consultant continued, 'We will do a blood test tomorrow, just because it has been under consideration. I'm sure it will be negative.' Delighted but disbelieving we waited for Monday impatiently, needing to know for certain. Maybe then we could get on with our life.

Two

The news

ДЭЭШЭЭ ТЭНГЭР ХОЛ. ДООШОО ГАЗАР ХАТУУ.
МОНГОЛ АРДЫН ЗҮЙР ҮГ

The sky is too far away. The earth is too hard.
Mongolian proverb

IT WAS A LONG WAIT until Monday. I was still reading about Down's syndrome and preparing my questions in case Billy did have it. I had worked in colleges and had seen students with Down's, but had never really known about their health background.

Although I was sleeping in a different ward, I was mostly in with Billy and someone had to push me in a wheelchair back and forth for my meals. I could not walk well because of the Caesarean, and the Neonatal unit was a long walk from my ward.

If any nurse or midwife came in, I told them about Billy and that started me crying. I did not know I could have so many tears, it was nonstop. That night, I finally dozed off after crying and reading up on the condition. I had an odd dream in the middle of my broken sleep. In my dream, a woman in a black gown with her head covered with a black scarf was carrying a baby in a car seat. Then she left the baby in a dump. The baby started crying. I ran to see if the baby was all right. As soon as I got to the baby, the woman ran off with a couple of toddlers following her. Then she turned around and I noticed she had a big long nose like a witch. I got frightened and woke up.

It was a horrible dream. It was then that I realised Billy would be like that baby in the car seat if we didn't accept him. He was our baby no matter what. My boy: born to me, to be my son. I told myself that whatever he had we would deal with it. I was trying to remember exactly what the consultant had said. Perhaps they were confused. Maybe they didn't have experience of a half-Mongolian baby.

On Monday afternoon we were taken into a small room with chairs around a coffee table. I was waiting for the news, the good news that Billy was a healthy boy. It was the opposite. The test had confirmed that Billy has an extra chromosome called Trisomy 21: Down's syndrome. I asked if Billy's brain and heart were all right. They said they were fine.

After asking if we wanted tea or coffee the doctors left us alone to take in the news. We stayed silent in our seats. It was hard to breathe. I felt numb. Richard stood up and walked to the window. He had his arms crossed, his body was swaying and he couldn't bring himself to say anything. Then he picked up the bowl of potpourri and sniffed it. It was a strange thing for him to do – normally he wouldn't even look at it – then he offered it to me to smell, saying, 'Nice.' He was desperately trying to make conversation after the long silence. Then we grabbed each other and started sobbing on each other's shoulders. What are we going to do?

We stood there for a while without words. Then we looked at the leaflets that the doctors had left on the table. There was a leaflet from Down's Syndrome Scotland with pictures of children with Down's. Of course, everyone was telling us about their experience of what it is like to have a child with the syndrome. But it was all such a shock. I certainly never thought that my baby would have any defects. I thought I was invincible. I thought it couldn't happen to me. I was wrong.

I went to my room in the hospital and rang the Down's Syndrome Scotland number on the leaflet:

'Hello, I had a baby three days ago. He was diagnosed with Down's syndrome.' I started crying down the line. On the other side of the phone I heard a gentle voice, listening to me carefully.

'Did you know that your baby had Down's syndrome before he was born?'

'No,' I replied. She said she would pass on my number to another mother who had a five-year-old boy with Down's. I felt a little bit better. I wasn't on my own.

Later that evening my mobile rang. It was Joanne; she had been given my number by Down's Syndrome Scotland. Joanne told me everything. Everything she had gone through personally, and also what they had gone through as a family. It was so comforting to talk to her. She said she had cried and cried and cried. Fraser was their first baby and she didn't know what to expect. She texted me the next morning: '… I remember giving myself a goal to pass a day without any tears.'

That text message gave me a huge strength. I got up and showered. I did my hair and put on my make-up. I walked

9

with my head held high – I was ready to do anything for my babies. I was ready for weeks, months and years of doing battle for my children, no matter what they had. Their mummy was ready. The ward matron saw me in the corridor. She said, 'You look great. You are a totally different person.' I remembered her when she first came in. I was in a bad mood, thinking, *What now?!* Just before she came in I had almost shouted at a woman who came in with a doll, trying to teach me how to breastfeed. 'I don't want to. I'm not interested. I don't even know if my baby is going to live!' I told her. The poor woman had left the room quickly.

Richard came to the hospital. He still couldn't tell my mum. He looked tired and low. He had brought a poem that Sara had written for me the previous year for Mother's Day, the day we found out we were expecting Billy. I'd asked for it, to remind myself that life doesn't end here.

My Mum
My Mum is the one who makes the sun rise
The one who does great things no matter how big a size
Her love has the power of a million shooting stars
She can go faster than any of the cars
She smells sweeter than the sweetest rose in the world
She is the one who makes the galaxy whirl and whirl
My Mum is the pretty and amazing grace
She can make the most perfect meals you can't resist to taste
My love for her is enough to go up and down to Pluto a million times
When she walks it sounds like the London chimes
The word Love is not enough to describe how I feel
Just one kiss can make anything heal
That's my Mum, That's my Mum.

Later that day I called my mum, who was at our home with Richard, Sara and Simon. I couldn't explain things to her properly. The term 'Down's syndrome' was not so well known in Mongolia. So I tried to explain about it, telling her that Billy has a disability. An extra chromosome that influences the whole body. There are different spectrums... My mum started crying. 'No, no, no. Not my girl. You have gone through enough in life. You can't suffer like this. You are on your own here without us. You don't have family support. How will you manage?'

It was extremely hard. I had never known or heard of my mother crying like this before. She too was in pain and unable to accept that her girl, her 'perfect' little girl, was going through this tough time. Like any mother she was trying to fix the situation, wanting to make things easier for me, but she couldn't. She didn't speak the language, and had never heard of the diagnosis. 'I'll raise him,' she said. 'I can bring him up in Mongolia.'

After talking to my mum I spoke to Richard, who was also worried about her crying and sobbing in front of the kids. Richard didn't want the kids to be worried. But my mum was being herself. In Mongolia, we live in a *ger*, a traditional Mongolian round house. A *ger* has just one room. We didn't know the concept of the word 'privacy' or 'personal space'.

I found myself torn between the two cultures. Richard was being himself and my mum was being herself. It wasn't anybody's fault. That was the way it was. I had to build a bridge between cultures, much as I had done over the years. But there are things that don't need interpreting. Human beings speak a common language when it comes to feelings. We were in pain together. We were hurting badly.

That night, I had another nightmare. I dreamt that Richard and I were taken into the same room where the doctor told us, 'There is one more thing...' I woke up.

The morning came, I went to see Billy. The doctor in charge asked me to let them know when Richard had arrived. At about 3pm, we were taken into a room. We felt sick inside thinking about what it could be, but we were also ready for just about anything. It had already started; we had to accept any complications that came with Down's. The doctor in charge spoke. 'We have found out that William has a hole in his heart. This defect needs to be closed. It's a routine operation. But for the operation, William's weight needs to be three to four kilos.' The doctor drew a diagram of Billy's heart and the defect. The gap was right in the middle of the heart. It was called AVSD, the abbreviation for atrioventricular septal defect. We listened quietly. We had no choice.

I talked to my dad and sister on the phone several times a day. My dad was working out how to come to Scotland. Even though he had just started a new job, he managed to take some time off. I thought it would be easier if my dad was here. I wouldn't have to worry about my mum being lonely and not speaking the language. They could talk to each other and be a comfort for one another. Plus my dad can understand medical terms and diagnoses to a certain extent. After all, he's been a vet for years.

After four days in hospital I was given permission to go home. Billy stayed in the Neonatal unit where we visited him every day, twice mostly. I had started breastfeeding Billy. I wanted to give him everything I could offer and treat him the same as Sara and Simon.

Before we left, a doctor said, 'It may not be so obvious that William has Down's because of your ethnic background.' I appreciated that she was trying to make me feel better, but I was annoyed. I thought, *Yes, but not all of my children look as if they have Down's.* So I put Sara and Simon's photo beside Billy. They could keep an eye on their baby brother. Also they could show people that you don't have to look as though you have Down's just because your mum is Mongolian. Anyway, Billy had ginger hair and paler skin. Later I joked that people would think I was Billy's nanny rather than his mum.

I came home and Simon and Sara were happy to have me back. Richard was relieved I was there to talk to. My mum was happy to have her daughter beside her. Then my dad came the next day.

It was a harsh winter that year, with a lot of snow, and it was windy most of the time. Richard and my friend Jackie took it in turns to give me lifts, now that Billy was at a local hospital, which was about 20 minutes' drive away. I expressed milk every few hours and took it to Billy, who was still feeding through a tube. We would have a cuddle, change his nappy and clean his face. After a couple of weeks I started trying to breastfeed him. He was a good boy, good at latching on, and he started feeding well. I returned to the hospital for a week before bringing Billy home. He was doing well until they checked his weight. He had lost weight. I saw one of the doctors in the corridor and started crying as soon as she asked how I was. We now had to bottle-feed Billy with special milk with more calories in it. He was losing weight because he was trying too hard when breastfeeding. Also he was on diuretics to help to get rid of body fluid.

I wanted to give Billy everything I could. I couldn't give him the medical care he needed in the hospital but at least I had been able to nurture him with my milk, and I longed for that closeness. When he moved on to the bottle, I felt as though my attempt to give Billy everything that I could had failed.

After I had been taught how to feed Billy with his special milk and give him his diuretics we were finally allowed to take him home, on 15th December 2009, a month after he was born. It was a beautiful feeling to be coming home with Billy. Jackie brought the two of us back. Richard was working that day and he had meetings planned – we still hadn't known in the morning if we would be allowed to take Billy home yet. So it was sudden but welcome news when we were told we could go.

Simon was over the moon to see Billy. He refused to leave him alone in a room even when Billy was sleeping. He was the big brother looking after his baby brother. My parents made a huge fuss, cuddling and kissing Billy. They cooked lamb soup for me every day. That is the Mongolian way of looking after a woman who has just had a baby. When I had Sara I was living with my parents. For a month I didn't do any cooking, washing or cleaning. I was looked after well. I was treated almost like a worshipped angel.

When Sara came home from school, Simon opened the door, announcing, 'Billy's here!' Sara rushed in and held him. She was delighted to see her baby brother. Nevertheless, she found it hard. She was old enough to know children with Down's syndrome. She couldn't look at pictures of children with Down's. It was too painful for her. She wanted her baby brother to be healthy. She struggled to come to terms with other things too. Her guinea pig had died the week Billy was born and she was only 11. My baby girl had grown up immensely in the past few weeks, witnessing life at its hardest. Now she shared her room with my mum. When my mum cried Sara reassured her, 'Granny, my mum will be fine. She is very strong. Don't cry.' In Sara's eyes I was strong, her strong mum with her kiss that heals everything.

A few days later, Richard and I took Billy to see Richard's mum Margaret in her nursing home. The nursing home was in our town and she had a beautiful view facing the sea. She was in a recliner chair, watching TV on her own. Her health had deteriorated rapidly; she couldn't even feed herself now. I got on well with my mother-in-law. We both counted ourselves lucky over the years. I was lucky that I had a mother-in-law who never poked her nose into our business. She was always there for me. I thought of her as my own mum and treated her as such.

We showed Billy to Margaret and she kissed him on his head. I held Billy facing into me, worried that she would notice Billy had Down's. She didn't know anything about Billy apart from the fact that he had been born. We hadn't told her about the Down's or the hole in his heart. We didn't want her to worry about us. Also, she was quite confused. She would remember things from very early in her life but not recent events, though she always knew who I was. We visited her every day in hospital until Billy was born. We thought life was tough then. Now, it didn't seem that bad.

●

We had appointments for Billy almost every day. He was under close monitoring. We had open access to the children's ward in one of the hospitals. I would feel such relief when the health visitor Mary visited. Mary was a deeply caring woman. She would compliment me on how I was handling Billy and the way he was growing. At first, my parents would go to the other room when she was around. They felt it was better to leave me to talk to her. They didn't really understand the conversation anyway. After a few visits, though, my dad was interested in asking questions about Billy. He would check Billy's weight with the health visitor and have a discussion through me.

Mum and Dad were a great practical help. Having just arrived from Mongolia, which is eight hours ahead of GMT, my dad would get up early because of the jet lag. He would look after Billy for a couple of hours while we had a much-needed sleep after being up during the night. My mum would look after Billy in the evenings until midnight. My parents were both trying to learn English and would test each other with their vocabulary. Simon and Sara's Mongolian got better while my parents were staying with us. Simon would ask for ice-cream, sweets and rice in Mongolian.

There were a few times when my parents' behaviour reminded me of myself when I came to Britain for the first time. They just disappeared to their room late at night on the first night. Richard said to me, 'Have they gone to bed?' I went upstairs and, sure enough, they had gone to bed without saying good night. It was a very Mongolian thing to do. 'Oh you are in bed. We wondered what had happened, and why you two were so quiet.' They burst out laughing. 'We forgot to say good night. Ok, we'll say it from tomorrow.'

Richard and I had had our cultural differences in the beginning, too, dare I say. Not long after we were together, he commented that I looked tanned. I was offended. I was so offended that I didn't talk to him for a day. Richard had no idea what he had done. Basically, he had insulted me. In Mongolia, girls try to look paler, and pale skin is considered pretty. Only country girls who work outside with animals look tanned. It is considered ugly. My parents used to give me a tub of face powder to protect my skin in the summer. They kept me indoors when the fierce sun was out and they were shearing our sheep. I was on cooking duties, away from the sun. After all that effort, to be told I was tanned was an insult.

Richard begged me to understand what it meant in the West. 'People here try to look tanned. It means they have money to go abroad, to go on holiday.' Richard continued, 'Some people even go to a special place to look tanned.' I didn't believe him until one of his friends agreed.

I also remember standing outside Clarks shoe shop when Richard told me to meet him outside Boots, the chemist. I had no idea there was a shop called Boots, which didn't actually sell boots. As far as I was concerned, Clarks was a shop that sold boots.

●

I thought I could take Sara, Simon and Billy to Mongolia. I could show them where their mummy is from, where she grew up and why she behaves in a certain way sometimes. I had a lot to tell them. I had a lot to show them.

I promised to myself I would do anything in the world for my babies, and Billy was our main concern now. We were thinking about the future. Who is going to look after Billy when we are gone? How will he be treated at school? Will he ever leave home and get on with life independently?

Richard and I were struggling. Richard had to work harder, especially now, with a disabled child. I realised that accepting Billy's disability was one thing, but dealing with other people's attitude towards Billy and us was a whole different story. My relatives in Mongolia were not told about Billy's Down's syndrome. The word 'syndrome' does not have a positive connotation in any culture, and anything wrong with any child is explained in different ways in Mongolia. One way is to say that it is the parents' fault, that they must have done something, by dropping the child, say, or that they are alcoholics. The other explanation seems to me rather dismissive and superficial. They would say: 'He is the reincarnation of so and so. That's why he looks different.' I couldn't tell my relatives yet. I needed my parents to understand it first. I needed to find the right way to talk about it so that people could understand and learn that it was not my fault. I wasn't afraid, though, that people would think that it was my fault. I have discovered that there are people and cultures in the world who know very little about natural causes. They need people to tell them about things, and show them how it affects people both physically and emotionally. These matters shouldn't be swept under the carpet and ignored. I needed to look back to my childhood and the very different Mongolian culture in order to move on in life.

THREE

Better than Lenin

Reach high, for stars lie hidden in your soul.
Dream deep, for every dream precedes the goal.

Pamela Vaull Starr

UNTIL MY SISTER ZAYA WAS BORN in 1984, I was an only child growing up in Uliastai, in the western reaches of Outer Mongolia. Both of my parents came from large families, with nine and eight brothers and sisters apiece, which meant that Zaya and I had seventeen aunts and uncles, not to mention their wives and husbands. Because I was a first grandchild for my paternal and maternal grandparents, all of those aunts and uncles spoilt me rotten.

Our traditional Mongolian house, known mostly in the West by its Russian name of 'yurt', was called a *ger*: portable, felt-covered, wooden-framed and circular. I later came to realise that while my parents moved around a fair bit in my childhood, the good thing about living in a *ger* is that wherever you go it's still the same house, the same home. Beyond that, our *ger* was special: not many were decorated as ours was. I loved waking up to the beautifully hand-painted support poles and above them the round *toono*, the single window at the top of the *ger*. Like the wooden poles, two columns and the *toono* frame were also hand-painted. There was something else, too: my paternal grandparents had seven boys and a girl, of whom my dad is the eldest; and grandfather told us that the beautiful big rug in the middle of our *ger* was bought by my grandparents when Dad was only 15.

Our home was also full of photos of me that had been enlarged in Russia, where my uncles and aunts had studied. This was during the socialist era of worshipping our Russian 'brothers' for helping us to rebuild a country and people that had for centuries struggled for independence from the Qing Dynasty of China. I dreamt of going abroad where you could get chewing gum, which was then a rare treat in rural Mongolia. My long ash-brown hair (fairer than usual for Mongolian children) meant that if any of my friends felt like teasing me they would call me 'Russian' or 'a cat' as an insult. Mongolians don't like cats. It's a superstition thing; they see dogs as honest and good friends to humans. But thanks to my uncles and aunts I was one of the trendiest children in town wherever I went, showing off my colourful Russian dresses and pretty ribbons.

Some of my happiest childhood hours were spent at an old desk, rescued from the school where my mum worked and now squeezed into our single-room home that already contained two metal beds, six beautifully decorated chests, a matching wardrobe, a yellow bookcase and a red kitchen cupboard arranged all around the wall. I felt very important doing my homework at that desk, with my schoolbooks and drawing implements. I even tried to make my own space by stitching a Russian poster of Lenin 'Bypassing Capitalism' to the wall hanging, beside the black German lamp that Father had brought back from Berlin in 1980. He was a vet, and had attended a professional development course in East Germany. I remember him bringing beautiful yellow leather boots for me and a television labelled 'Wesna' from Moscow, on his trip back. The television was a great attraction to my uncles and aunts and after meal times in the evenings our *ger* became something of a cinema.

Until the mid-80s we had only Russian programmes to watch – with my dad mostly interpreting for us – and I was so embarrassed at the sight of a man and woman kissing that I pretended to be reading or doing something else. Russian culture was much more open than ours. When Mongolian broadcasting reached into the rural areas, it was a great feeling to watch our people speaking their own language and playing our music. Those early programmes were taped and brought to our town by plane as it was impossible to broadcast to the whole country at the same time. Broadcasting via the Asiasat satellite was still to come in the 1990s. We watched the news and everything else three days later than Ulaanbaatar, the country's capital. But our programmes were more restrained than the Russian ones, so I no longer had to hide my embarrassment.

My desk area was perfect for me to ignore what was going on behind me and get into whatever I was doing after my household chores. Reading became a passion, and my favourites were novels and short stories. My parents told me that I 'lost my ears' when I read. They had to come and physically close the book to get my attention. One night, I nearly burnt the *ger* down trying to finish a book. The lamp was too close to my dad's radio and its glass front melted from the side. This led my parents to ban me from reading anything other than schoolbooks.

I had to learn to switch off from the outside noise when concentrating on my studies. There were no other rooms where you could go. The *ger* has just one room, serving as bedroom, kitchen, living room, dining room, study room and just about any other room you would know in the West. So it was useful to learn to concentrate on my studies when my parents were chatting to each other, my sister was toddling around, the TV was on and most of the time we had other relatives or friends dropping by. The *ger* has a stove right in the middle; as you enter it is facing towards the right side, and the chimney faces the opposite side, where the guests are normally seated. In some rare cases it is reversed in order to divert the evil spirits, which might happen if, for example, a family had been trying to have a baby without success.

In my carefully arranged office area I began to write poems and short stories. My first poems were titled 'My Dad's Work' and 'Teacher Lenin'. Even when I was very young my parents had great expectations for me. My mum was a teacher of Mongolian and Literature and our house was full of books. She used to read me stories whenever she could.

Sometimes I would ask Dad for a story and he would start with: 'Once upon a time there was a little bird looking for a nest. He decided to build a nest for himself and started carrying a piece of grass from far, far away.' Then Father would stop. A few minutes later, I would ask, 'How about now?' He would say, 'Still collecting more.' Eventually, a few years later I was fed up with his usual response of 'Still collecting more', so I said, 'Please finish the story when I'm older and driving a Volga in Leningrad.' Of course, he was happy with that and probably relieved that a nagging child stopped asking for a story to which he did not yet know the ending himself!

By the time I was three my parents already expected me to go to university. They had both been themselves and, in the socialist era, were proud that I was growing up in a family that could classify its background as *seheeten* (meaning both parents had been university-educated) on official papers, whereas their own background had been from *ajilchin* (working class) and *malchin* (herdsman). I was the first generation in their families able to claim that I was from a *seheeten* family.

My parents had had their lectures in Russian and Mongolian. My dad had had to learn Russian well as most veterinary books were in Russian. So when some of that language rubbed off on me my parents showed off my language skills to any visitors who called in. My Russian vocabulary consisted only of words for mama, papa, broom and window, but my mum told me I would be a very clever person and she expected me to be famous, even better than Teacher Lenin, she said.

We weren't allowed to mention Lenin without the title 'Teacher'. Our school was full of socialist quotes and translated Russian slogans: 'All for one, one for all!', 'Long live socialism!' and 'Learn, Learn, Learn.' We used to march every year on May Day, celebrating the international labour movement, and in October we celebrated the Bolsheviks coming to power. Mongolia's first winter snows usually fall in October. Every school, every nursery and everyone else was expected to march through the small square in Uliastai and wave to local dignitaries, who were standing on a smaller version of the mausoleum in Moscow, beside the communist flags. I remember it being a long wait for a short walk past these important people, and feeling so cold that we jumped up and down to keep warm – all for people who waved back with hands in black leather gloves.

●

Uliastai was one of the five big towns in the western region of Mongolia, and the centre of Zavhan province, which itself is larger than countries like Scotland and Austria. Outer Mongolia was a Chinese province between 1691 and 1911, and Uliastai was the western 'administrative centre' for the Manchurians who governed China. Their derelict ruins were just a mile from my parents' *ger*. We would sometimes go there and find all sorts of things. We lived in one of the '*ger* streets' in the north of Uliastai near the river Chigestei. Collecting water was a strenuous job. We hauled water from the river all year round, apart from some spring times when the snow melted and the water quality was poor. We also had wells at different points in the town that people could use. And water trucks would come at certain times, sounding their horns: I would haul about 20 to 30 litres of water each time nearly every day. The distance varied depending on whether we wanted water for drinking or washing. Drinking water was about 2km away whereas washing water was about 1km from our home. At other times hauling water from the river also became a social activity. We would go with friends to fetch water, and the four or five of us would play and chat endlessly on the green riverbank. In the summer we used to wash our clothes and swim. After swimming we would lie on the sand or stones beside the river drying ourselves in the sun, telling stories in turns.

In winter the frozen river became our skating rink. I didn't own a pair of skates, but we would borrow from one another and take turns towing each other pretending that we were figure skating on television. We would wear tall felt boots, so tall you could almost sit on them while wearing them. We would tie the loose skates to our felt boots and try to skate, falling over countless times. I wasn't really good at it. The felt boots made you feel as if you had put your legs in a pair of wooden pipes. So moving in them was quite hard and looked funny, especially when they were new; I felt like a toddler trying to walk. After a while they started to mould into the shape of our feet.

●

In my pre-school years Mum took me to work with her, teaching Mongolian and Literature. I loved the Literature classes. It was like listening to bedtime stories. I often hid under my mum's desk. I don't know why, but I suppose I may have been told to. The pupils knew and saw me under the desk. The other teachers and the head teacher knew I was in the class. It's odd that I couldn't just sit beside the pupils. My parents took me out of kindergarten because they said that every time I went I came home with something like a runny nose, if not diarrhoea. Besides, I was probably one of the most rebellious children my kindergarten teachers had known. I remember having an awful tantrum one day and demanded to go and see my mum in the school next door to the kindergarten. The teacher said, 'You can't behave like this here, even if you do with your parents.' I was answering back, 'So let me go and I'll do this where I can do it!' screaming and running towards the door. I think my parents felt guilty too. So there I was beside my mum, under the desk listening to the biographies of authors around the world and information about world-famous works of literature, including those of Pushkin, Tolstoy, Chekov, Shakespeare and Goethe.

I used to itch to talk when it came to term exams. The pupils would come one by one beside the desk and tell my mum what they knew of specific authors and their works. My mum was assessing them. I would answer their questions in my head and then wait to see if they would match my answer. It was frustrating if they didn't. I have to admit that once or twice I gave them a clue and the whole class burst out laughing. They were 16- and 17-year-olds. So I guess it was funny being tutored by a 5-year-old.

Being a teacher's daughter meant I was well known in the school, so by the time I started my first year I was *Suvd bagshiin ohin* – the 'daughter of teacher Suvd'. When my sister Zaya was born, I was seven and I started school – a year younger than my classmates. I wanted to go and I had already tried going when I was five. On that occasion, my parents had to ask a teacher to let me sit in class for a few days. I was already reading and I begged them to send me to school. So I had a go for a few days but I got only *Dund* – average marks. I wasn't happy with my marks and left. My parents were relieved. They were not even that serious: they didn't buy me a uniform. Anyway, this time it was different.

Four

Long live socialism!

*The ruling ideas of each age
have ever been the ideas of its ruling class.*

Karl Marx

THE SCHOOL YEAR for about a thousand pupils ranging from 7 to 18 years old started on 1st September. After a month of school days we would have a couple of weeks out to help with autumn work. All of the classes were allocated work. Communist labour was deemed to be a great deed and an opportunity to shine like a true model communist. It could be anything from harvesting vegetables like potatoes, cabbages, turnips and carrots to sawing wood and chopping logs or preparing hay in the farm. In the early morning we would gather outside the school with our work clothes and packed lunches, waiting for the trucks to come for us to climb aboard. It was exciting to start with, but then after a few days our hands and faces got drier and our enthusiasm would drop. The nice bits were that we used to play during the lunch break and sing on top of the trucks and turn people's heads in the streets. Sometimes boys would throw marble-sized potatoes to get our attention.

There was spring work, too. We used to bring water in two 10-litre containers from the river and water the trees in the school area and pull out weeds throughout the town. I remember the biggest communist work we ever did. Uliastai had a dumping ground in one of the valleys near the town. One spring the whole town went to work there. The first week we dug holes. Massive holes were created making small hills. The next week we put the rubbish in the holes and covered them with soil. We worked hard, sweating in the dirt and dust. Every organisation in town came out and helped, until the site was rubbish-free and fresh.

Our school had a special team of children who went around the classes checking everyone's cleanliness. These were 'Zad Ugaagch' – the team name translated as 'Squeaky Cleaners'. They would come into the class and take a row each, ordering us to take off our shoes and be ready to get our toenails checked. We also had to put our fingers on display on the desks for nail inspection, and show our clean, ironed handkerchiefs if asked. Our hair and clothes were also examined for lice and nits. If the class did well we got a red flag for a week and could feel pride in ourselves. If we did badly it was tough news. The Zad Ugaagch team would choose a couple of the dirtiest children and put a big picture of a pig around their necks. The most embarrassing part was that these children then had to do a tour around the school visiting every class, and the pupils were encouraged to laugh at them and say, 'Be ashamed of yourself.' The poor kids with their big badges would be almost falling over, hiding behind each other. I guess it worked, for many of them were determined not to have to do that tour again.

I went to school with my youngest uncle, Eendee, who was just a year older than I was. My grandmother died at 49, leaving my grandfather with nine children aged from 3 to 26. Eendee was 3 and his brother Geegee was 5. My mum was the second eldest and the oldest girl. She became the mother to her younger siblings. Eendee and Geegee lived with my family for a few years. Geegee started school and that's when I learnt to read, following him like a shadow. My poor mum had to shoulder all the motherly duties. The good thing was that my grandfather was not poor. He was the only child of a horseman who kept horses that were famously fast in Naadam (the big annual Mongolian festivity).

Life was hard in the socialist times, with many families struggling to get by. We would queue up early in the mornings for meat and milk outside a small wooden kiosk on top of a little hill in the centre of our district. Although herdsmen had milk and meat, they were not allowed to sell these openly. This was considered to be a capitalist thing to do and was therefore illegal. Everything had to be supplied by the government and local authorities, and everyone had to have the same food and drink. But there wasn't enough of either of these in the system. The shop shelves went empty and the Mongolian government had to introduce a ration-card system depending on the number of family members. The card allowed families to have flour, sugar, rice, matches and tea bricks. My parents both worked full time in good jobs and we always had plenty to eat. If we did struggle my parents made sure I was not aware of it. We weren't having jam or *moloko* (Russian custard) every day, but there was enough bread, butter and granulated sugar for breakfast and lunch. For dinner, beef or mutton was plentiful, and there was always some rice or flour to make pasta and pastries.

I would take a 1-litre container at about 7am to the wooden kiosk to mark my place in the queue. Even at that time of day I wasn't the first there. Some people would come, put a stone marker down and go home to bring their containers. We would wait for hours while playing games, guessing the number of marble-sized stones in our hands and coming up with film titles from abbreviations of letters. Sometimes children brought their basketballs and skipping ropes. We had great fun playing games until the milk or meat trucks came, when there would be chaos. The strongest mostly got what they wanted first and I would end up being behind this chaos watching them fighting to get a litre of milk or a kilo of meat, too scared to be involved in case I got crushed. If my uncles or aunts were with me it was easier. They would dive into the crowd and battle their way and come out with a heroic grin and milk or meat for me. It was survival of the fittest.

Some families started to make flour at home using hand mills consisting of two flat round stones with a hole in the middle. I remember visiting my grandparents. They didn't have to worry much about buying milk, but flour, sugar and tea bricks were hard to find. I remember having my turn with the stone mill, making flour in my dad's parents' house. They would bring a sack of wheat or grain and fry it until it was brown. Then once it was cool we put it into the hole of the mill and ground it carefully. We had to have a rhythm to do that. The grain started to become uneven if we rushed it. My grandparents were not pleased if they noticed that we were mucking about and not doing it properly. The big, uneven parts of the grain would make it impossible to chew. Even so, the flour tasted rather like Weetabix cereal.

It was hard for many families with empty fridges, and the whole family would often go all day without anything to eat until it was dinner time. Dinner for many families was the same thing: a few strips of meat and some flour sprinkled with salt. I was lucky to be born to my parents. My dad got a job as a deputy chairman in the Food and Agriculture Authority in Zavhan. As such, he was responsible for managing both wild and domestic animals in the area; with his jeep and driver he would travel the region for weeks, visiting every *soum* (village), checking how they were doing raising animals and planning for the winter.

I used to miss my dad and I would clamber onto on his lap as soon as he came home. He would come in smelling of wild chives, petrol and cow dung smoke. I loved that smell. I often smelt my dad's shirt when he was away and my mum would make jokes. 'Oh, your dad probably smells of cigarettes and sweat.' I found comfort in this smell. My dad used to bring frozen rounds of milk in winter. The Mongolian winter is so cold that milk can be frozen in a container and when taken out it keeps the same shape as the container. In the summer he would bring butter squeezed in a sheep stomach and milk in containers. Sometimes, if he went to the southern *soums* where they were well known for homemade sweets, he brought back fudge for me.

My parents were both '*ulaan* (red) communists' as they called themselves in a jokey way. The term '*ulaan* communist' meant that they worked hard and for long hours, leaving their family and children behind and just concentrating on their work. They would come home late at nights. They worked six days a week. On Saturdays they finished at 3pm but it was a rare sight to see my parents come home before 9pm and indeed sometimes they didn't come back until after 1am if a meeting went on late. These meetings were about planning the next five years' work or reviewing the last five years' work. My parents would warn us they had their *tardaggui hural*, which translates as 'endless meeting'. We survived because my aunt Daidaa got married and their *ger* was beside ours in the same fenced area. My grandfather also moved his *ger* there. So Zaya and I were not alone. But it was still my job to look after her when she was little, and I remember jumping up and down on our metal bed, which was my way of rocking her to sleep. But I was only little myself. Zaya would laugh or cry depending on whether she was scared or enjoying the movement. I also sang to her, looking through the *toono* – the only window on top of the *ger* – noticing that it was getting darker. Sometimes my parents found that Zaya and I had fallen asleep with the TV on and the door locked from inside. I kept the TV on to keep us company.

FIVE

Girls go bald

Most men live like raisins in a cake of custom.

Brand Blanshard

ZAYA LOOKED LIKE A BOY after her head was shaved when she was four. This is a Mongolian custom, with boys getting their first haircut at three or five and girls at two or four. We had a ritual almost like a wedding. My parents prepared a special pair of scissors and then decided who should cut Zaya's hair first. The person should be selected carefully according to the horoscope. Zaya was born in the year of the Rat, so the person who is suitable would have been born in Dragon or Monkey year, with a four-year gap from Rat year on either side. My dad, who was born in Dragon year, started the ceremony. The pair of scissors was tied to a blue scarf, which is used in religious rituals and traditional customs. Zaya looked so cute as her hair was cut by everyone after Dad, accepting their presents graciously – including toys, sweets, clothes and pencils – with a huge smile on her face. Once everyone had cut their bits of hair, my dad shaved Zaya's head. She looked surprised to see her naked head, but she enjoyed the attention. It marks the point at which a child is considered to have survived the dangers of infancy. Before this, parents do not cut their child's hair.

There is a certain sitting order and place for everyone in these kinds of rituals and weddings: women sit at the right side of the *ger* and men at the left, all according to their age, starting with the eldest. The eldest would sit at the north of the *ger* opposite the door. Our *ger* was full of relatives and my parents' friends that day. I loved having people around like this. My parents and my aunts had prepared food including lamb noodle soup, dumplings and rice pudding. My dad was responsible for serving vodka in small shot glasses. He sprinkled some in the air with his ring finger and touched his forehead in prayer. The guests then each accepted the glass in turn, with the right hand outstretched and the left hand held under the elbow of the right, took a sip, and passed it back to my dad using the same gesture. Then my dad would top it up and offer it to the next person. Everything including food was served starting from the eldest. My job was passing the food and tea between my mum and the guests, using my right hand or both hands. It is considered to be rude to use our left hands to give and take things from people.

After a few rounds of vodka the guests started to sing, mostly folk songs. The person who was about to sing was given a shot of vodka, holding it until they finished. Others joined in, usually from the second line, and the whole *ger* filled with singing. Then some drank it all and some sipped the vodka and gave the remainder back to my dad. All day they ate and sang and made jokes before going home later in the evening.

I didn't get my haircut ceremony. I think I was born at the peak of socialism, when everything traditional was deemed to be bad. Many families had to hide their worshipping ways and do it secretly. We know that a neighbour of ours had burnt down their *ger* because they had lit a candle beside a Buddha hidden by a photo frame.

●

Every year on the 11th and 12th of July, the Naadam festival takes place all over the country. Every city and every village celebrates the *Eriin Gurvan Naadam* – the 'Three Manly Sports'. These are wrestling, archery and horse racing. If you don't know any of the wrestlers it can be boring. In the capital and bigger towns, wrestlers qualify according to their wrestling experience. But in the countryside that does not count as much. If you want to wrestle you just have to put your name down. The wrestlers get matched in pairs regardless of their height, weight or build. They wear a *zodog* and *shuudag* – traditional wrestling costumes consisting of a pair of short trousers and a long-sleeved shrug (an open-front top, demonstrating that you are not a woman), both embroidered and made from silk. They also wear traditional Mongolian hats that have pointed tops. Before wrestling they leave their hats with the *zasuul*, a person who is there to give support whenever needed. He usually sits cross-legged on the grass and watches his wrestler while holding his hat. The wrestling rules seems simple for people like me, but complicated with methods and strategies to people who are really into the sport. Whoever touches the ground first with their knees, elbows, shoulders or head is the loser. So they stand there pushing, pulling, tugging and dragging, trying to make the other wrestler fall to the ground. It is a knockout competition and there are usually nine rounds. But the final four rounds are the ones we watch with most interest.

The archery is well organised and of a higher standard only in Ulaanbaatar. In Uliastai, of the three Manly Sports, it's the one that attracts the smallest crowd. My favourite sport is the horse racing. Although I didn't ride in races like my mum and my oldest uncle Baabaa, who both raced without saddles, shoes or helmets, I loved following after the horses in a jeep on my dad's lap. My dad had to work during Naadam. His job was to follow the races in a jeep and be on hand in case of accidents. There are no paved or purpose-built race tracks in Mongolia: the race courses are open countryside. Another of my dad's duties was to give the signal to start the races. When it was roughly the right time for each category according to the age of the horse, he would blow a trumpet, causing a huge panic. The horses and the kids riding them would start to gallop, leaving a huge cloud of dust in the air. We would drive beside the races over a dirt road up and down, left and right, avoiding potholes and dubious edges with nobody, of course, wearing any seatbelts. I would hold onto the small metal bar in front of me, bouncing up and down on my dad's knees. I was thrilled to be there as it would feel that we were racing as well. The jeep used to have a big red flag on top to indicate that it was the one authorised to give signals. I wasn't that thrilled to see some children falling off their horses, though, with the blood running down their noses or next to horses that lay twitching. The children who fell off were picked up and checked by doctors, whereas looking after the horses was my dad's job. The children used to be more upset that they couldn't finish the races than noticing that they were hurt.

Horse racing was also an occasion for parading. In Uliastai the racing took place a few miles outside the town in the mountains. Many trucks and jeeps were loaded with people in their best clothes, mostly newly made *deels* and new clothes bought specially for Naadam. All day, while waiting for the horses to come to the finishing line, people had a great time eating, drinking and playing all sorts of games. We ate *huushuur* and *buuz* – traditional Mongolian dishes made from meat including mutton, beef, horse meat and *gedes* (the stomach of a sheep or goat). It was fine and relaxing, with the general smell of food in the air while we enjoyed being out in the open. The sky was always blue, people were happy and many of us wished every day could be Naadam.

In 1988 my parents moved to a different *ger* district with the nickname Gegder Tsudger (meaning 'the ones with bellies and snooty attitudes who are in managerial roles') in Uliastai. There were no other *gers* beside us and we kept about five white goats to get the milk for my mum, who was not well at times because of her liver. I never knew what the diagnosis was. White goat's milk is considered to be good for the liver in Mongolia, so Zaya and I learnt to milk them. Sometimes my dad did a little bit of hunting for birds and animals, to help my mother feel well. She tried eating different meats: rabbits, different type of birds and marmot liver. At times, my mum would have to stay in hospital for weeks. Then, Zaya and I would go to my dad's work and wait for him in his room while he had meetings elsewhere. We would fall asleep on the chairs and then be carried into the car and go home with my dad. It felt empty not having our mum at home. She was the one who made sure we had food and snacks. So I started to learn to cook with Zaya. We cleaned the house together and I was glad I had a sister. We sang while doing our housework together and we had a great laugh. We would try to sing as if we were in a choir, starting at different points and then making mistakes, getting the other person confused with their lines. As we were 'just the two us' we were encouraged by our parents to look after each other.

At summer holidays, we would go and visit my grandparents, who had moved outside Uliastai. Sometimes we walked and sometimes my dad would borrow a motorbike and all four of us would travel on it. I was the big girl and sat right at the back, with my mum and Zaya sitting behind my dad. We didn't wear any helmets and the road was rocky and bumpy. Once my dad stalled riding up a mountain and rolled back. I fell off the bike and managed to get away before the bike rolled over me.

I used to get scared of dogs when we passed other *gers* on the way to my grandparents. The angry dogs would race after motorbikes especially, and bite at our legs. My grandparents would have many of us to stay during the holidays, my cousins and us taking turns. We were there to help with the animals and with gathering cow dung for the fire. I was the first grandchild and I used to share my grandmother's bed. She would sniff my head showing her affection and giving me kisses and cuddles. I would do any housework that needed doing before they asked me to. My cousins were a couple of years younger than me and most of them were boys. So they would wrestle outside the *ger* and we had competitions supporting our favourites.

My uncles and aunts and my cousins would bring different food and treats to my grandparents, but there were always too many of us to be really satisfied. In the mornings we would have our deep-fried bread, two or three each depending on how many there were.

I have to admit I was hungry sometimes when I was with my grandparents and pretended that I wasn't well. That trick worked. My grandparents had to let me go home by stopping any cars passing by and asking if they could take me. I recovered quickly when I got home where there was more food.

Later in the 80s, people began to question socialism. Herdsmen started to sell milk and meat and we didn't have to queue at all. The time was changing. The pro-democracy protestors in Ulaanbaatar were starting to wake up Mongolia.

SIX

How do you start your fire?

*Happiness doesn't depend upon
who you are or what you have;
it depends solely on what you think.*

Dale Carnegie

SANT, MONGOLIA, 1990. Six hours after leaving Uliastai, we were driving cross-country through the Bor Hyariin Els sand dunes, by way of a short cut. We were separated from the truck carrying all of our worldly goods, including our dismantled *ger*, which had to take a longer route. As we reached the top of a sandy hill, the landscape revealed a small village on the bank of beautiful twin lakes. My parents were beaming as they pointed at the village and announced to me and Zaya, 'That's Sant, and the lake is called Holboo Nuur.' Holboo Nuur was actually two lakes separated by a narrow causeway where horses and cars could cross. Sant itself was a small village with a few fenced yards called *hashaa*, most of which were empty as the families had moved to their summer locations. Some of the yards still had *gers* inside and some had small wooden bungalows, hand-built in different shapes and sizes. In the middle of the village stood the wooden post office, a few buildings where the local authority officials worked and a club called *Soyoliin Tov* – the cultural centre. Dirt tracks trailed through the village, coated in dust and sand unlike the dust and small stones in Uliastai.

Our new home was on the southern side of the village, behind the tiny hospital and next to a small power station that supplied the local community. There were four buildings there, making eight semi-detached houses arranged in a horseshoe shape, with some space in the middle for us to play. Our house was at the end, on the left, near to the Naadam stadium and the trench toilets. The houses were painted an orangey-pink colour and the doors were green. Our house had been newly decorated for our arrival, and we could smell the strong odour of paint as we arrived. It was exciting to explore our new permanent home in a new place: ours had three rooms and a long corridor with double doors. The big room was used as a living room and the small room became my parents' bedroom. Zaya and I slept in the big room on a felt mattress on the carpet. The third room was the kitchen with a log-fire stove in the corner.

The news of new arrivals travelled fast and soon we were invited to have traditional tea and dumplings called *buuz* with different families, and, as can happen in the remote Mongolian hinterland, most of them seemed to be related to us. I was overwhelmed by the welcome these relatives and friends gave us.

I made friends with a girl called Booyo, who was two years younger than me and whose mother and stepfather worked in the same company as my father. Soon we discovered that we too were actually related through our mothers. Booyo's great-grandmother and my great-grandmother were sisters. Booyo was a beautiful girl who turned heads in the street. In Sant everyone knew everybody else, and being friends with Booyo, as well as the daughter of a newly appointed chairman of the agricultural cooperative Baysgalant Amidral ('Joyful Life'), my dad's new job and the main reason for our move, I soon became as well known as others.

There was no postal system as such and people from other cities and villages wrote letters addressing people by their surname (actually, their father's first name), then their first name. In the Mongolian postal address convention the person's names come last.

So the address looks similar to this:

Zavhan aimag (province)
Sant soum (village)
Boldbaatariin Bat (addressee)

The letter or postcard finds its owner by being passed from one person to another, which might take a day or possibly a few weeks. It was not unusual to hear the two post office workers asking people if they had seen anybody from such and such a family because they had a letter to pass on.

Only a few families had telephones and they were mostly the ones in the *yagaan baishin*, the pink buildings. Zaya and I used the phones mainly to arrange our trips to the river or Holboo lake with our friends. We would take washing with us in a basin and head for the water. Booyo would come with us and we'd spend hours swimming and listening to pop music on a tape player.

●

The new school term started in the autumn. On 1st September 1991, I started my 7th year, aged 14, at the only secondary school in Sant. The school consisted of a few buildings with classrooms and dormitory accommodation for pupils from the nomadic herdsmen's families. The rooms in the boarding school were nicely decorated by the children, with their little embroidered curtains hanging in front of their metal beds and brightly coloured duvet covers. But when I visited these rooms I always felt sorry for the younger children, living away from their parents, missing home so badly. I made a few friends in my class, most of whom gave the impression of being related to me. I wasn't so sure after a while, because sometimes people wanted to be related to my family on account of my father being the chairman. People started to refer to me and Zaya as *Dorj Dargiin ohid* – 'Chairman Dorj's daughters'. So my name was changed for me from Teacher Suvd's daughter to Chairman Dorj's daughter.

The company my father managed had over a hundred thousand animals, including camels, horses, sheep, goats and cows, all collectively owned. These five animals are the main livestock in Mongolia. If anybody refers to livestock, it means these five animals. I remember when Zaya was visiting us in Scotland. She was talking about the five animals and couldn't remember the word for one of them in English while talking to Richard. She asked Richard, 'What is the fifth one?' Richard hesitated and guessed, 'I don't know, is it pig, chicken? ... erm ...' Zaya was hysterical. She was laughing so much that tears were coming down her cheeks. She expected everybody to know that there were a certain five animals. Richard had no idea why she was laughing so much.

So my father represented one of the two most senior positions in the village. It seemed my father was in charge of the animals and the herdsmen in the village. If anyone wanted to have a sheep or a goat for food they came and asked for his signature. They had to write a letter requesting what they needed, and what for. I knew the system very well, because I acted as the 'scribe' for many of these letters. People would come and ask Dad for permission to slaughter an animal without a letter. If he was home they would turn to us and ask for a paper and a pen. Some people plainly did not know how to write the letter, whereas others just preferred to have me write it for them, dictating what to say: 'My son is getting married. Therefore our family would be grateful for a sheep and a goat to supply the food for the wedding'; or 'My mother is feeling poorly. She needs to have hot soup to make her feel better. We would be grateful if you could kindly support us by providing us with a sheep.' Then I would date it and the person would sign it. Father's signature was the final decision. Sometimes, he refused if he found out that the reasons were not genuine.

My mother was now teaching at my new school. With her philosophy that anyone could do anything, she loved teaching, and knew how to link learning with practical life. She praised children till they were pleased to do their homework, surprising some parents who saw their children memorising long poems studiously. Mother also knew how to engage children in learning. I was one of her pupils and I was always well prepared for my classes. My classmates would look at me to check if I had done my homework or not. I tried not to embarrass mum in front of the other children by not having done my homework. If I hadn't done my homework she couldn't have asked other children to do theirs.

In 1991, with the collapse of the Soviet system, the Mongolian government reintroduced the traditional Mongolian script known as Uighur. Mother took great pleasure and satisfaction from the fact that the native language was once again to be taught in schools. The writing, which reads vertically from top to bottom, had been used until 1940, when the socialist governors changed official Mongolian writing to the Cyrillic form of the Russian alphabet, which still remains the governing Mongolian script.

Mum taught children how to make ash boards in her classes to help them learn to write in traditional Mongolian. I remember my classmates trying very hard to make their boards look beautiful using wood and sunflower oil, before sprinkling some ash on them. Then we used wooden pens to write. It was a great experience, learning to write the traditional Mongolian that had been used for hundreds of years.

This was a time of transition, with democracy getting underway and the Mongolian economy still shaky; things were getting worse in some areas and were particularly difficult for some families. Father started going to the Chinese and Russian borders on behalf of the village, taking raw materials such as cashmere, wool, hides and meat. He would take loads of animal-based materials to trade with the Chinese and the Russians. He brought back mainly tea bricks, sugar, flour, tape recorders, dried apricots and plums for the villagers. From China, he brought home a nice big music system with coloured lights that went on and off in circles when the music was on for the family. Our old record player became redundant. He also brought a cooker with an oven and a nice shiny display cabinet from Russia for the living room. Mum filled the cabinet with pictures of Buddha and her ever-increasing collection of china. She loves collecting ornaments, usually bought in pairs: 'Just like our two daughters,' she would say. The cooker worked well, but we didn't know how to operate the oven or what to bake or cook in it, so we kept the sugar and bread in it.

One day I went to babysit for a relative in the shanty *ger* district in Sant, among rows of fenced yards. While looking after the baby I let the fire go out in the stove. As it was wintertime, the *ger* quickly felt cold and I decided to rekindle the fire. I looked everywhere and couldn't find any paper to start it with. Luckily, the baby's grandmother popped by to see how I was doing. She told me to use a thin slice of rubber from inside a tyre to start the fire. The smell of rubber filled the *ger* and it was awful. I could not believe that they didn't have any paper to start their fire. I realised I didn't know how hard life could be, and how poor some people were. It became even more noticeable at lunch time. Again, I couldn't find any food apart from some meat and flour. The grandmother saved me and the baby that day. She came back and started making what looked like a cake mix and then fried it in the wok. It was delicious. Again it made me think. At home I was used to having deep-fried *boortsog* bread all the time. There was never a day when I had to think about what there was for me to eat.

My parents had old magazines, newspapers and notebooks for starting fires and our shed had sacks of flour and sugar. We had a couple of paper barrels of dried apricots and apples in my parents' room. My mum was always very kind to people. She would fill children's hands with sweets and dried fruits. She would tell us to be kind to everyone, that it does not matter how they look or what they have. She was so kind that people loved visiting us and we had visitors all year round, day and night.

In Mongolia, anyone can come knocking on your door at any time of day. Having studied in Ulaanbaatar, my parents had friends everywhere in Mongolia. It was common to have our door knocked at 3am in the morning, when people who were travelling stopped by for something to eat and a bed for the night. I often had to wake up from a deep sleep and start making noodles. I used to get annoyed at first, getting up slowly, not so keen on feeding people in the middle of the night. That changed when I started going to Uliastai to study for my last two years at secondary school. I needed a bed and food while travelling in the cold for long hours. After that, I would jump out of bed and readily cook and make beds for people who happened to be passing by.

In 1992 things started to change everywhere as all the Soviet-era State-owned animals and properties were being privatised. My dad became the last chairman whose job it was to privatise all of the animals and the animal sheds in the countryside in Sant. It was a massive job. They counted all of the animals and the members of every family. With nomadic herdsmen, he had to work out where each spent the winter, spring, summer and autumn, so that animal sheds could be given to those who already used them. Of course, some people were unhappy if they were allocated weaker animals or they didn't get exactly what they originally wanted. There was no way that my father could please everyone, and that was when we saw who our real friends and relatives were.

Just like everyone else, my family had been given our own animals. I didn't have much experience of animals; in fact, my grandmother had called me 'no eyes for animals' because she thought that I had no idea what to do when it came to looking after animals. That summer we took our *ger* with some basic furniture, leaving everything else in the house, and moved to Bayan Davs – Rich Salt Area. Sant has three areas: Bayan Davs (Rich Salt), Bayan Ulaan (Rich Red) and Bayan Nuur (Rich Lake). Each area is divided into territories, and the herdsmen are allowed to look after their animals within their own territories. Bayan Davs was named Rich Salt because it had a lake that produced salt. This had been a major income earner for Sant. Now it was not a State-owned resource and consequently there was no coordinated work on it. Some individuals would go deep into the lake using a hand sieve to try to fill a sack. It looked like hard work.

The only water fit for human and animal use in Bayan Davs came from wells. My parents erected our *ger* on top of a small hill beside the *gers* of my father's uncle and two cousin's families. We were about half a kilometre from the nearest well, a cement-lined hole in the ground with a wooden cover. We used a rubber bucket at the end of a long rope to pull up the water. Zaya and I were on duty, bringing water home in 60-litre containers, rolling it up the hill and having a little rest in the middle while admiring the stunning nature around us. We would sit on the grass gazing at the beautiful deep-blue sky, so stark and cloudless and painting a striking scene above the low-lying hills.

We each would water the animals every couple of days or so. Because our four families kept their animals together we could look after them in turns, using a rota system. The sheep and goats, which totalled over a thousand animals, had to be distinguished from family to family. Our goats had blue paint behind their horns and the sheep had a horizontal blue line across their bellies on the left side. When it was our turn to look after them, Zaya and I walked all day following them, making sure they didn't get mixed up with other herds in the steppe or on the mountains.

Sant is in the desert region, where the Mongolian summer is very hot, reaching almost 40°C, with few trees to provide shade from the fierce sun. When it's that hot, the goats stand on higher ground, facing into the wind, and the sheep all stand in a circle burying their heads in the middle, huffing and puffing. Zaya and I would sit down and have some of our *tseedem* mixture of water and a few dollops of yogurt and eat *boortsog* bread and *aaruul* – dried curds. We would sing and play card games and sometimes I would read stories to Zaya. In the late afternoons, we would slowly guide the sheep and goats towards our *gers*. We would then wait for our parents' signal to come home, leaving the sheep and goats nearby to make their own way home. My parents' signal was to put my mother's red dressing gown on the sloping roof of the *ger*. We would smile with relief to see the dressing gown so bright against the white *ger* cover, dancing in the mirage.

Coming home to our dinner waiting for us was the proudest moment of the day. We felt we deserved to be treated with respect after looking after the sheep and goats all day. There is a strange saying that Dad used to repeat: 'The person who looks after sheep needs food, the person who looks bald needs a hat.' Mum would then treat us like guests, putting food in front of us and looking proud.

People in Sant generally seemed to prefer boys over girls. Boys were thought to be stronger and more suitable for heavy work outdoors. Apart from riding horses and looking after sheep and goats, boys were thought to be more independent. For those reasons, many boys dropped out of school at an early age to look after livestock and it was mostly girls who went to school, especially after the privatisation. I was pleased that I didn't make my parents feel bad about having girls, and was determined to show people that I was not weaker than the boys.

Zaya and I learnt to ride horses and could drag a sheep or a goat along in each hand when it was milking time. All of the ewes or goats with lambs and kids needed milking. We would look after the lambs and kids separately from their mothers all day and, before they were put back together, we milked the mothers. Zaya and I raced with other children, tying the sheep and goats in a row using ropes; they were interlocked head-on like clasped hands in order to keep them still for milking. We had about seventy goats and thirty sheep to milk by hand into a bucket. Once the mothers had been milked they were released from the rope line and their kids and lambs were allowed to come and meet them. We were supposed to milk the mothers so that we left some for the young offspring. The noise of the ewes and goats meeting their lambs and kids was very loud, each of them calling to their own.

There was a lot of competition between the children of different families. From getting up in the morning till going to bed at night, we were in some sort of contest at all times. In the mornings families cleaned their metal chimney by taking it away from the *ger* and banging it with a long-handled brush. Sometimes it worked if you just tapped the chimney gently from the outside, repeating all around it. That noise basically signalled to other families that we were up and about. In the summer, we had to get up before sunrise to milk the cows, before they started wandering off to the steppe for the day. The more considerate ones would moo loudly reminding people that they are running late. Once the cows were milked we had to clear the dung from the area. I remember putting my hands in warm cowpats to keep my hands warm. We would stack the cow dung over the dry cowpats we had already gathered, building a mini-pyramid the size of a *ger*. Cow dung was used as fuel once it was dried in the sun and the smell was like incense for us.

In the countryside, nomadic people could not carry around fridges in the summer when they were moving about following the best pastures. Even if they could have, there was no electricity. So Mongolians were self-sufficient and enterprising. We dried our meat after cutting it into thin strips; these we hung on a line like a washing line and we smoked them with cow dung. It is called *borts*. The taste is fantastic. We chose which sheep we wanted for food from the herd. The meat was organic, free-range and chemical-free. My parents would decide on the animal, and some of us, Zaya and me included, would dive into the herd to catch it. Usually the fattest was chosen and held down while the person who was slaughtering it would cut a narrow slit in the chest first. Then a man (only men do the slaughtering) would put his hand through the slit into the chest cavity and tear the aorta. It is considered to be kindest for the animal and the blood collects inside without spilling out over everything, including the skin. As children we were not allowed to see this process.

Once the sheep was dead, Zaya or I would help to hold down the legs while the animal was skinned and its stomach emptied. When he was younger, Father did the slaughtering, but older men don't do it, perhaps because killing animals is considered to be a sin and they hope to be reborn as one of the nicer animals. Mum would clean the intestines while showing Zaya and me what to do.

Around Naadam time in Sant every family would prepare *shine shol* – a fresh soup made just after a sheep or goat had been slaughtered for food. Naadam was different in Sant from in Uliastai. The horse racing was easier to watch because they raced around Holboo lake, whereas in most places the race would disappear off into the countryside for a couple of hours. I would sit on top of our shed beside the stadium and watch the race through binoculars. Naadam was a great excuse to meet up with classmates and friends from different parts of Sant and have parties. The thing I most enjoyed was dancing in the club. As soon as I graduated from my 8th grade in Sant I was allowed to go to the dance. My parents made a huge fuss of me going to these dances. Mum would bring out the most colourful *deels*, which were hidden away in suitcases on top of the wardrobe. My dad would climb up a ladder to get the suitcase and they would watch me doing a fashion show in front of them. They were very proud of me as I was growing up and following in their footsteps, preparing to go to university. After all, in their eyes, I was getting closer to being famous and even better than Lenin. Having said that, my parents were good at bringing us down to earth when it came to discipline. They would threaten me and Zaya: 'Well, if you don't try hard at school, you'll have to become a herdsman's wife and look after our sheep and goats. We pay people to do it, why can't you two end up doing it?' The thought of being stuck in the countryside killed me. I wanted to travel the world; I had bigger plans and I wasn't going to stay in the countryside looking after animals.

Dancing in the club was the only way for some young people in the countryside to meet others or be noticed. So women young and old made a huge effort in putting on their make-up and wearing their best clothes, including bright colourful *deels* and dresses with their high heels for graceful dancing. In Mongolian culture, if someone is tall, confident and beautiful they are described as being 'like a deer'.

The men who went to these dances were mostly in their late teens and early twenties. There were some keen dancers among them who were older and came along and danced every dance, showing off their shiny shoes and clean, crisp white shirts with newly pressed trousers, and letting us all know what aftershave they had put on. The younger ones were mostly dressed in traditional Mongolian boots or Russian army boots, strutting around in a deliberate manner as their body language announced that they feared nothing. They would stand with their boots carefully creased down and polished for the dance. They had long satin belts casually wrapped around their body over their *deels*, but dangling down across their hips, top buttons undone – it was their way of being rebellious. They wore their caps at a jaunty angle, walking as though in a slow dance, dragging their feet across the floor, moving as if they had a hedgehog under their armpits and moving their heads as though they had a neck-brace on. They would compete to invite girls to dance. I was one of the first girls to be asked and I thoroughly enjoyed the attention, dancing to waltz music played on the only Casio keyboard in the village.

Once the main festivities of Naadam were over, the third day eventually became part of the holiday, when groups of people would get together for day trips. Work colleagues, friends and families would all gather nearby at a river or lake and have a barbecue. The 'barbecue' was different from the usual way of grilling meat directly on the fire, and very unlike Western barbecues. Large round rocks from the river were heated on the fire, and then added to chunks of fresh meat, boiled with wild herbs, and cooked for hours, while the delicious smell permeated the air. We would play cards and other games as we waited. Sometimes the card games evolved into people running around in wet clothes and laughing their heads off. The punishment for losing at cards was to be thrown into the water; then the losers would try to drag the winners with them into the water. The weather at that time of the year was always sunny and dry, so nobody minded the soaking.

When the barbecue was ready, the hot rocks were passed around and we held a stone or two until it finally became cold. Holding hot stones and rubbing them gently over exposed parts of our skin is still thought to be therapeutic and good for us. The meat cooked in this way fell apart in our hands, and is the most scrumptious I have ever tasted. Of course, the favourite drink, vodka, is passed around, too, in shot glasses. Sometimes, we would have fermented mare's milk – *airag*. It's fizzy and savoury and about the strength of beer. When my father was a vet I remember going around with him to different families who made *airag*. You could tell from the outside if the family were making it or not. The clue was having mares outside their *gers*, tethered to tall poles.

Talking about vodka and *airag*, I learnt to distil vodka at home. We began by putting homemade yogurt into a container over a few weeks. The container was kept beside the stove and Mum would add a few bowls of sugar now and then. We would stir it until it hissed and bubbled. Mum showed me how to do it. Dad was waiting happily to test my first attempt at home-made vodka, sitting with his legs crossed, cigarette in hand, tilting his head and closing one eye slightly. I put a big wok on the stove first and poured some of the fermented yogurt into it. Then I put a tall aluminium cylinder upright and evenly balanced into the wok. Mum had prepared a little pan to collect the vodka. This pan was suspended inside the top of the cylinder held by strings weighted at one end by a small hammer and the other end secured to a small axe. Over the pan we put another wok that had never been used on the fire, so it had a nice clean bottom, perfect for distilling the vodka into. Once the yogurt boiled, the vapour hit the small wok and heated it. Cold water poured into the top wok condensed the vapour into liquid, which trickled into the pan. After repeating this process a few times, my vodka was finally ready. My parents were both excited. I lifted the pan and the smell of the vodka filled the *ger*. My parents suggested testing it by dripping some onto the flames of the fire in the stove. I splashed some into the stove using a small ladle and it burst into flames. My parents praised me for making my first successful vodka. Word travelled fast and our neighbours came in to taste it. Father had the first taste and nodded, saying, 'Strong' with pride in his eyes. He passed around my vodka to the neighbours in a small silver bowl with carved dragons on it and they all agreed how good it was.

When autumn approached, Dad started hunting marmots, small rabbit-sized animals that live on the steppe. Marmot skin was exported to Russia for a good price and the meat was rich in taste. Father had a very funny outfit for hunting marmot. He would wear Mum's old white dressing gown, a white sun hat and old cream-coloured shoes. Then he had a stick with a fox tail on it that he would wave around while walking on his toes and making noises like the marmots, who would be curious and stand on their back two legs responding to the noise. At that moment Dad would shoot them down. He didn't shoot any marmots that were not standing up as he thought they might not be healthy enough. Dad would always take care to check the meat before cooking as marmots are carriers of bubonic plague.

Sometimes, I would meet Dad in the hills to bring the marmots home on horseback. I would come home with about five carcasses hanging from each side of the saddle. I hated their fleas. I would feel this nipping sensation on my body and sense the little beasts deep in my skin, diving in for a good suck of blood. I used to scratch at them furiously and flick them onto the ground. In the morning, we would skin the marmots. Zaya was good at it and she liked doing that sort of thing. I tried a couple of times, but ended up making holes in the skin, which didn't go down well with Father, who was hoping to sell the skins to traders. The meat, usually boiled, was tasty and the fat stayed fluid like sunflower oil. It didn't go solid like sheep or goat fat. Sometimes we burnt off the fur to get rid of the fleas, stuffed the marmots with hot rocks, and cooked them over an open fire. Marmot is also considered to be medicinal. People would swallow the heart or lungs raw and still warm after being shot. One of my friends knew an older hunter who squeezed the fluids from the gall-bladder into his eyes. He was in his 80s, and had been doing it for 50 years, claiming that was why he could still shoot marmots!

Zaya and I learnt how to clean the intestines of goats, sheep and marmots, one of the skills that country people thought it was important for girls to acquire. Others included learning to make *deels* and boots by hand. Mum was very good at fashioning anything from almost any piece of cloth. Zaya and I had the most beautifully finished clothes made from her or my dad's old *deels*. I particularly liked a green *deel* that had been made from one of my dad's old ones. He had burnt a cigarette hole on it, but Mum embroidered beautiful flowers around the hole and people thought that it was deliberate to make me look prettier. The flowers were on the right side in the front. Mum also made fine trousers for me using her old skirts and putting buckles from my old sandals on the waist and at the back, looking very trendy. I have never made a *deel* for an adult, but I have tried to make my underwear by hand. There was nowhere to go and buy girls' underwear, so Mum gave me a lot of material, mainly white cotton. Then she taught me how to make bras and knickers for myself on our sewing machine. So I learnt how to do most things apart from making boots, ticking all the boxes towards becoming a country girl who could one day make someone a perfect wife.

SEVEN

Leaving home

*Leaving home in a sense involves a kind of second birth
in which we give birth to ourselves.*

Robert Neelly Bellah

'THAT'S YOUR BED.' My uncle Adia pointed at the bed on
the left, on the chimney side of the central stove in their
ger in Uliastai. Their *ger* always looked clean and tidy, with
nothing out of place or any rubbish cluttering up the home-
stead, and the hand-painted wooden furniture looked just
perfect there. Adia is the fourth of my dad's five brothers and he is probably the shortest and shyest of them all.
His wife, my aunt Ombo, is just the right match for him
– quiet and never raising her voice. They have a daughter
Altai who was then about five. She was a pleasant little girl,
not spoilt, always trying to please her parents. Adia worked
at the Post Office in Uliastai town centre and Ombo stayed
at home, doing the housework, hard work that is not considered work at all.

My mum and I had come to Uliastai a few days before the start of term at my new school, Secondary School Number 1, to settle me in. Mum came with me as she is a teacher after all and she knew a few teachers from my new school. Dad and my sister Zaya stayed at home in Sant, Dad in his now not-so-new job. Zaya was starting school that year, the same year that I was leaving home to finish my secondary education, for the last two years before going to university. I was looking forward to starting at my new school; it was like going on an adventure, leaving home for the first time. With my new brown uniform and white smock, with its matching crisp white collar, and my freshly washed hair and feet, I was ready to start my new school on 1st September 1992.

Mum left a few days later, once I was settled in my new class, 9B, which was a language-based class. Luckily, my main class teacher was my old teacher from my previous school. Teacher Nadmid had taught me Russian for two years in Secondary School Number 2 and had this year moved to Secondary School Number 1, which was just a stone's throw from his flat.

Our class had 22 pupils and they came from different *soums* and schools in Zavhan. Our classroom was on the second floor, facing south towards the Eldev-Ochir monument. The school was actually named after Bat-Ochirin Eldev-Ochir, a Mongolian politician who was born in Zavhan in 1905 and was seen as an exemplary communist, becoming head of the Internal Security Directorate during the socialist time.

There were six classes for our year, and pupils were chosen carefully after an entrance test and an informal discussion with the class teachers. We were classified according to our different subject interests using Cyrillic letters: 9A were the Maths brains; 9Б were the Chemistry students, the white-gown wearers; 9B were the language experts, with many tangled tongues; 9Г were social sciences, the historians; and, finally, 9Д was the economics class, filled with 'look at me' boys who would swagger down the long corridors past our classroom door. Being a language class we were mainly girls, with just five boys. The five boys sat at the back and 'watched' the girls over the two years. I sat just in front of the boys in the right-hand row with Nasa, a gently spoken, shy girl from another *soum*, Erdene-hairhan. She was good at her subjects and she became my new best friend.

After introducing himself formally, Teacher Nadmid stood in front of us and, while throwing a familiar glance at me now and again, introduced the school do's and don'ts. Being in the company of hormonally driven boys and girls bubbling with the excitement of starting a new school was overwhelmingly thrilling. The language class meant we had more hours of Mongolian, Russian, Mongolian Literature and Traditional Mongolian than the other classes and fewer of the other subjects. English was the new hot spice in the pot. It represented many opportunities in my eyes. Teacher Dari taught English to us after her two-week teacher-training course in Ulaanbaatar. She brought with her a pack of newly published English course books called *Blue Sky*. My English then was zero. Nothing. Not a word. A few weeks in and I was repeating after Teacher Dari, 'How are you? I'm fine, thanks. And you?' mixing my 'p's and 'f's just like everybody else in the group, calling myself 'pine' and Nasa my 'priend'. My journey in speaking English started with no idea of where I would end up in the world.

Our Mongolian teacher was called Bolor and she had the most colourful eyelids we'd ever seen. They looked as though a rainbow had landed on her eyes and stuck there permanently. This dolled-up teacher was one of the best teachers of Mongolian we'd ever had. She was passionate yet strict in her delivery and inspired us immensely. She liked Songo, another of my newfound best friends, a lot. Songo wrote poems and read widely, so she'd argue and debate with the teacher while enjoying the attention. Songo would entertain us with her infectious laughter, which was a one-off. It echoed round the classroom and had a light feminine inflection that brought to mind a film in which a beautiful girl had just seen an attractive young man and was drawing attention to herself in a flirtatious way.

Our classroom had a record player that was built into the inside of the teacher's desk. During break times we would play this catchy record by Sofia Rotaru, a Russian singer, and show off by opening the classroom door to let the other 'poor' classes hear what we had. Sometimes, the boys would ask us to dance with them and we would have fun dancing between the yellow desks that were nailed to the floor.

Soon the cold winter arrived and the journey from Adia's *ger* was difficult to do at times. Every morning Adia and I got up at six o'clock and caught the bus about 7am. As the *ger* doesn't have any windows other than in the middle of the circular roof, we had to go outside to check if the bus was coming or not. Adia's *ger* was in Maltai Horoo, the direct translation of which is 'a district with animals'. It was a few miles outside Uliastai, on a country road, which meant there were no street lights and no bus shelter. The only clue we had that the bus was getting closer was when we caught sight of its lights, or when we could hear the sound of its bigger engine, which was different from any cars that there might be. Once the bus arrived, children and adults would race to the only bus stop in the district and try to get on. My classmates Nasa and Songo also travelled from my district – Adia's *ger* was in the street between their streets, so we could call to each other over the wooden fences – and they got on the bus with us. The bus was often pretty well full up with schoolchildren at that time of day and we mostly knew who went to which school in Uliastai. At the end of the journey we got off at the terminus and walked for about five minutes to school. Sometimes the bus didn't come at all and we then had to walk for an hour over dirt roads and hills covered in snow and ice. That meant we were late for school, coming into the classroom with our eyelashes frosted and our red cheeks glowing.

The school we went to had a reputation in Zavhan for its posh pupils who lived in flats in the town centre. A paler complexion and cleaner look with shiny shoes seemed to be the norm. Well, till I started that year at least. I wore my old felt boots that winter, thinking them one of the finest-equipped and warmest of boots. They were bought by my parents, who told me they were excellent boots, with their leather patterns around the front and back and a sole attached nicely to prevent holes developing at the bottom. So, living away from my parents, I now didn't have to worry about fixing any holes myself. At home, our felt boots often used to get holes in them and my dad would fix them while sitting in front of the fire, sticking them together with melted plastic. Later on, superglue came on the market, which saved burning fingers and the awful smell of hot burning plastic.

One day, my two friends and I were walking out of the school to the bus stop and heard a couple of teachers chatting behind us. 'Look at that! What on earth has come to this school?! The standard has slipped in this school.' 'Oh, I know. It's getting worse.' We were shocked and surprised and looked at each other and at my boots. Then, as usual, we knew what to do – we started laughing out loud so as to irritate the toffee-nosed teachers till our paths separated. Nasa and Songo were soulmates really. We had so much in common in terms of our values and attitudes, and we never, ever bad-mouthed anyone. Waiting for the bus at bus stops and walking long distances strengthened our friendship and I settled into my new school just fine.

I wasn't at the top of the class, but I was happy that I was coping with my studies. Living in Sant had meant that my Russian had got worse because we didn't have a proper Russian teacher there. The teachers were not always qualified, and our Russian class was not as challenging as I would have liked. Teacher Nadmid was surprised to see how much behind I was. When I was his pupil a couple of years previously, I'd been one of the best in the class, but now I had slipped back badly. That made me quieter in class and I was happy to sit at the back and just get on with my work. I was focusing on my homework, hoping that if I could cope with it, it meant I was doing all right.

My bed in Adia's *ger* had a beautifully embroidered blanket case that sat decoratively on the metal bed during the day as the blanket was folded like a roll and fitted into the case and the bed was used for sitting. The bed itself was covered with a lovely soft green quilt and the front was decorated with a frilly white embroidered banner hiding whatever was underneath. This kind of decoration was the fashion then. Every family had these embroidered blanket cases to keep their quilts, blankets and pillows tidy during the day when they were not in use. The embroidery was mainly flowers, with patterns in all shapes and colours, sometimes illustrating years of special occasions like the Olympics – with words like 'Москва 1980' (Moscow 1980). Ombo was good at embroidery and Adia and she were houseproud people who took good care of what they had and spent their money carefully. After all, they had only one salary coming in.

My parents had asked me which family I wanted to live with before I joined Adia's family. Even though my grandparents and my grandfather lived in the same street just a few *gers* away I chose to live with Adia. The main reason was that Adia and Ombo lived a quiet life, which would suit me for studying. I also had a soft spot for Adia, who was gentle and kind to me. I knew Ombo would never tell me off. My parents made sure they supplied sacks of flour and meat for the year to the family to cover my expenses. This was also good for Adia's family as the time of rationing still existed and, without extra rations, Ombo might have had the added pressure of not letting me go hungry. The truth was I was never hungry. I would go round to visit my other uncles, grandparents and grandfather's family, who were all in the same street, and I accepted any food on offer. Many evenings I didn't have my dinner at Adia's because I was already full. I well remember the time when Ombo cooked *bantan*, boiled flour in water with a few strips of meat, spiced up with a pinch of salt. I thought I was not spoilt, but I was and I didn't like having the same thing for dinner every night.

My parents would send me deep-fried *boortsog* bread now and then with a hand-written letter, written mostly by my mum. The first letter and *boortsog* arrived not long after I started at my new school. I sat beside my little *avdar* – the wooden box where I kept everything including my clothes and money – and started reading. '*Sain baina uu, minii huu? …*' Tears started rolling down my cheeks and filled my eyes so that I couldn't read the next bit. 'Hello, are you well, my child?' This was nothing more than my mum would normally say, but written this way, so far from me, missing me, as if she knew I was missing her, these words had the power to make me sob, so much so that Ombo was worried and came to pat my head while fuelling the fire, which was already full. Eventually, I calmed down a bit and plucked up the courage to finish the letter. That letter was the most precious thing in the world to me. I kept it in my little plastic bag where I kept the sacred red thread given to me by a local lama and read it from time to time, hiding from people so as not to show how much I missed my home, my mum's cooked meals, my dad's smell and chit-chat, my little sister's sweet face as she followed me everywhere, keeping me company and trying to do everything I was doing. At times, I felt like running away back home. But I had to stay. I had a mission to complete. After all, I needed to do well and look after my little sister. That was my own mission in my head: the big sister needed to show her little sister that she too can do the same – go away to study and become a grown-up who can do everything and be independent.

Adia worked as a mail sorter now. His previous career as an electrical technician with the Post Office had ended when he'd fallen from a rotten post that broke at the bottom, leaving him with epileptic seizures. Before then, he had trained in the army in sending signals using Morse code and had worked as a communications locator. After the fall, he'd had to fight for his job and eventually the Post Office had given him a job in the sorting department. It was hard for Ombo when Adia had seizures, especially at night. We all got up and tried to hold him down to prevent him hitting his head on anything or hurting himself in a fall. It was upsetting at first but I soon learnt different ways to hold him down, helping Ombo, and when he took longer than normal to come round, I ran to Maama's house for help. I banged as hard as I could and Maama knew exactly why. He would answer, 'I'm coming,' and appear within seconds. Maamaa is my dad's third brother and his house was in the same fenced yard as Adia's *ger*. Maamaa is a carpenter. He made his own furniture before his wedding, as well as some of Adia's before his. In fact, they got married the same year, one in the spring, the other in the autumn. Maama's wife is Aaga, the most pleasant person I'd ever met. She was a pharmacist and she came across as intelligent and warm. Maama and Aaga got married in a house that Maama and my relatives built, rough-casted, painted, cleaned and decorated, whereas Adia and Ombo got married in a brand new traditional *ger* my grandparents had prepared. Maama and Aaga had a toddler son called Davka. Maama's house was really handy when it came to waiting for buses in the mornings. Having windows on the side of the house meant we could watch the bus lights appearing from inside, in the warmth, then rush out.

My longest time away from home came to an end and I packed my bag to go back for the term-time holidays. I missed home madly and desperately. It had been a full two months, the slowest two months of my life. I prepared some sweets for Zaya, a packet of cigarettes called Marlboro for Dad and a pair of woollen leggings for Mum. It was the best feeling ever when I clambered into a truck cabin to start my journey home with three men from Sant. The three men were going back after a business trip to Uliastai and my parents had asked if they could bring me home for the holidays. We had 360km to travel on a country road with no street lights or signposts. We set out on our journey about 7pm on a November evening. With a temperature of -20°C during the day, dropping to -30°C at night, I wore five layers of clothing: a pair of tights, three pairs of woollen leggings and a pair of jeans over it all, along with my treasured felt boots, a few pairs of socks and a few layers of warm clothing inside my sheepskin *deel*, which I had borrowed from Ombo.

I was ready to go home to see my dear parents and my lovely sister. I fondly imagined my parents would give me kisses on my cheeks; they would have prepared my favourite food including *buuz* and fresh country cream with Mum's home-made deep-fried *boortsog*. She would have sprinkled some sugar in it to make it even tastier. I dreamt of Dad asking me questions about my new school, while holding the cigarette I'd brought for him between his fingers, tilting his head and smiling. I thought about Mum running round bringing out things she had kept, bought or made for me. Zaya would be shy at first, just looking at me. Then she might want to sit on my lap or play with my hair, starting to show that she had missed me. I could imagine grabbing her and giving her a big kiss on her forehead. Her bald head. Actually, she was not that bald any more. Her hair had grown since the traditional shaving ritual and she now had fine little pigtails. Maybe she would be taller now. Two months is a long time. I knew that I would feel the love as soon as I touched the door handle and opened the door. I couldn't wait. It took twelve hours, they said. We will be there the next morning when they are just getting up. The drone of the truck lulled us into the night. I fell asleep.

Suddenly, I woke up when the truck stopped. It was pitch black, but the sky was filled with a spectacular display of stars. 'We are lost.' The driver slammed the door and went outside to check where on earth we were. 'We've been round this hill three times.' 'I thought we'd gone back on ourselves,' the others muttered. I looked at the stars and noticed we were heading in the opposite direction from our destination. 'We are going backwards,' I declared, '*Doloon burhan*, the seven stars.' I pointed at the sky. They didn't take my word for it. The driver drove on. I had seen the stars every night when I went to the trench toilet before going to bed. The stars symbolised to me that life is magnificent, and that it does not stop here in Uliastai or Mongolia or even on the Earth. I was familiar with the pattern and position of these interesting bright stars, and I knew where the tiny ones mostly appeared. I fell asleep again.

I woke up when the truck stopped again. This time we were in front of an empty shed enclosure for animals. It was full of dung, which meant it would be warmer than being in the open. The three adults pulled out a tarpaulin and put it down as a groundsheet, then we used the rest of it as a blanket, wrapping ourselves in a huddle to keep warm and settling down for a few hours' sleep. The men decided to wait till the morning rather than wasting even more petrol not knowing where we were going. The cover was cold so we shivered close to each other until we finally fell sound asleep.

The next morning we got up and had some ready-cooked *tsuivan*, which is a Mongolian stir-fry, basically a mixture of beef and noodles with a few strips of onion with a clove of garlic tossed in. Once fed, we drove on and eventually reached Sant in the late afternoon. My parents and Zaya were over the moon. I felt like the queen of the universe eating my favourite *buuz* and sipping salty milk tea in my warm home surrounded by my nearest and dearest. Heaven.

The holiday passed by quickly. I went back and forth a couple of times more during school term times, and made it to the spring, when the first year away from home was over. Just before the school holidays my dad's family was struck by a tragic incident, though. My father's oldest brother, Gana, one of the friendliest of my uncles and the head teacher in the secondary school in Sant, was killed. What hurt most and shocked us all was that he was hit on the head with a metal pole by the husband of one of the teachers. He had advised the teacher to work temporarily in the boarding school till she got her job as a primary teacher. She wasn't happy and went home and cried and told her husband about it, who then waited for my uncle the next morning around a corner from his home with a metal pole in his hands, consumed with rage. My uncle died a week later. He got up after the incident and did his normal work for the morning but went to see the doctor as he had a bad headache. The doctor checked his eyes and told him to lie still. He lost consciousness there and then. He had told the doctor what had happened before he lost the ability to communicate or do anything. That was the first time that my family had lost anyone this way. Gana left his wife Dash with four children aged 5 to 14. It was a terrible shock. Who would have thought there was more to come?

Eight

Dancing wolves

Чоно харвал хиймор сэргэдэг.
Монгол ардын бэлгэдэл үг

Fortune smiles on you when you see a wolf
Traditional Mongolian saying

IN THE SUMMER OF 1993 we moved to Bayan Nuur, an area with lots of lakes and rivers. It was a pleasure to have so much water. Previously, in Bayan Davs, we had had to use the one bucketful of water for as many things as we could. It started with doing the dishes or washing something light-coloured, and usually ended up washing the floor. But in Bayan Nuur our *ger* was quite literally just a stone's throw from the river. That location was the most beautiful place. I still daydream myself to sleep imagining myself in our *ger* on the carpet, hearing my parents' happy whispers, with the comforting sounds of the sheep and goats calmly grazing, the peaceful rippling of the river and occasionally a distant dog barking.

Our *ger* was right between the river Hungui and the Bor Hyariin Els sand dunes, which we would slide down, racing each other and rolling so that our clothes and bodies were smothered in sand, still laughing. We then jumped into the river; it was a great time. Here we didn't have to look after the sheep and goats that much, as our neighbours who shared the responsibility had five boys around our age. So they were good at doing anything for us and enjoyed showing off their horse skills and their sturdiness.

Their parents and grandmother were secretly hoping that I would go out with one of them. At any opportunity, they would tell me anecdotes about their boys and how good and charming they were. After a couple of years the grandmother must have lost hope, especially after I started university. She would say, 'There isn't anybody in this valley that is equal to you.' Her compliment referred to the fact that I was learning foreign languages and was anticipating travelling the world.

One year, our neighbours made felt at the riverbank. It was like a ceremony. For several weeks beforehand, people were invited to come and help. They had many boys and they needed a lot of felt for covering their *gers* for when they were to get married. Our neighbours brought out loads of sacks of sheep's wool and scattered it all on the riverbank. We were given two thin sticks each and had to hit the wool until it became fluffy with no tangled bits in it. Then they sprinkled water all over it as if they were watering flowers and put another thin layer of the wool on top. Once this had been repeated another couple of times the whole thing was rolled up around a large, long pole. The pole had long ropes attached to the ends so that it could be pulled along by a horse or tractor at speed. The rolling action acted like a centrifuge, compressing the teased wool into felt. While the horse or the tractor pulled the pole, making the felt, we had food and drinks outside beside the river. It was a warm communal feeling. Passers-by would stop and give us a hand and then continue their journey. We all knew each other, so there was no feeling of awkwardness. And if a stranger came by, they would often come to talk and have something to eat and drink before continuing on their way.

We used dried dung for fuel. I know we could have afforded to buy logs and coals if we had wanted, but using dung was something free and that was just the way it was. We would put a light wicker basket on our backs and a long rake-like tool called a *savar*, made of thick straw-coloured wood, pur-pose-built to go under a dry cowpat and pick it up, leaving any dirt or soil on the ground. At first I had a rotten aim, with dung going everywhere, but I soon got the hang of it, happily chucking and swinging the dung over my shoulder into the basket without looking. I actually enjoyed collecting dung as it gave me the freedom to think and be in my own company. Another indication of a hard-working family: the pile of dung-fuel outside their home. A big dung collection was a sign of a well-organised family. It could rain for days, so plenty of dung meant a warm home and freshly cooked food on the stove. There is a special food we made on rainy days. It was tea with rice, salt, butter and sometimes *borts* (dried meat.) It was one of my favourites, and you could feel your body warming up as you ate the hot food, almost like some sort of therapy. It was not good if the rain was com-bined with a strong wind. The sand dunes looked as though they were on fire, with sand blowing all over the place and the sheep and goats became frightened and disorientated. They ran everywhere panicking, especially if there was any thunder and lightning. In the summer, we didn't use fences, and the animals were just left outside without any shelter. Most days were all right, but days or nights like this were a nightmare.

I remember being woken up by a loud clap of thunder and the sheep and goats running off madly. Zaya, Dad and I put on our wellies and raincoats and went out to round them up. We couldn't see more than a metre in front of us, but, holding our torches, we managed to find the herd and we stood there with a long stick catching any sheep or goats that were trying to escape. The occasional flash of lightning actually helped us to see what was happening in this mayhem. Dad was worried that the wolves would seize this opportunity to attack, so he blew his *doon* – a white instrument similar to a conch-shell that made a noise like a trumpet. This noise is supposed to frighten away the wolves as they can't stand this sound. After a couple of hours, dawn broke and things calmed down. We just hoped the sheep and goats were all there as it was impossible to see exactly how many there were.

The next morning, my parents and our neighbours counted our sheep, goats and cattle. The news was that three lambs had been taken by wolves that night. It was scary to think that I might have been standing beside a wolf in the dark. As the day got brighter we went out to scan the dunes using our binoculars. Father spotted a massive wolf on one of the dune hills watching over the herd calmly. He brought out his gun and shot into the air a couple of times and the wolf jogged off into the wilderness, leaving us alone. Although they were a constant threat to livestock, it was considered lucky to catch sight of a wolf. So my parents made sure that we all got to see one in the hope of a lucky future.

●

Summer was a nice season and it was easier to look after the animals then, although the heat caused problems. Temperatures could reach 40°C. Some sheep, goats or calves developed itchy bottoms as flies tried to land on them. They would move their tails madly trying to swat the flies away and rubbing too hard to relieve the itching, they would end up with red, scarred skin. That attracted insects and flies even more, and grubs found their way onto the raw flesh. Cleaning the grubs was one of the things I didn't like doing. Zaya and my dad usually held them down on the ground and picked the grubs off with tweezers one by one. Then they put iodine on the wound and let the animal go. Sometimes, families had no idea how to get rid of them as they multiplied so fast; my dad was often called to check animals in the neighbourhood to see if there was anything wrong.

In 1993, after my summer holidays, I went back to Uliastai for my final year at secondary school. It was easier this time, as I knew what I was doing and I looked forward to seeing my classmates. Adia and Ombo had moved their *ger* to the town centre in Uliastai and now shared Ombo's brother's fenced yard. Ombo's brother had two sons and we all got on well. Nasa and Songo moved too, and they were close by, which was particularly convenient for our friendship. Songo's mother was a nurse and worked shifts. Then Nasa and I would go to Songo's and spend the night to keep her company. Adia wasn't very happy that I was staying away, and he would sometimes come late in the evenings, calling my name outside the *ger*, admonishing me and telling me to come home. He probably thought we were with boys and could be in bad company. In fact, the three of us cooked, then read poems and listened to Songo singing and playing the guitar. Songo would have her own poems in piles, but she wouldn't show any of them to us. She would say, 'You'll read them when it's time,' meaning her book will eventually be published and we would read them all then.

◦

I always came home in winter to help my parents with the preparations for Tsagaan Sar — the Mongolian New Year — which was celebrated in January or February depending on the lunar calendar. There were three main preparations for Tsagaan Sar. The first was making meatball dumplings wrapped in a thin flour and water-dough pastry. My family made over three thousand dumplings. Word would spread that we were making our dumplings on such and such a day and relatives and friends would gather. We would all have different duties, with some people flattening the dough using rolling pins while others pinched the flat dough and wrapped minced meat inside. As I was one of the youngest I was on rolling-pin duty. By the end of the night, my palms had turned red and all I wanted was to have a rest. Once they were all done, though, we had the tasting of the dumplings, with lamb noodle soup. It was a great social activity as people would chat endlessly about all sorts of things including jokes, films and books. It often turned to local gossip, with discussions about who was marrying whom and everyone adding their own titbits.

The other preparation for Tsagaan Sar was making long pastries like biscuits or scones, rectangular-shaped with rounded corners similar to a shoe sole. They were piled up in an elegant display with sweets and dried curds on top. My mum predicted how the next year would end up depending on how well these delicate scones had turned out. Again, people were invited to help, with some kneading dough and some making patterned scones using special hand-carved wooden kits. We made about 70 of them and kept them uncooked overnight until they had more or less dried into a shape. The next morning, our job was to make sure the chopped wood for the stove was thin and the right size, and my mum would be on a massive mission to deep-fry the pastries in the same shape – flat and unbroken. She would stand there for hours, paying attention to every detail; she was hugely disappointed if one broke or had an uneven surface. One of the tricks we learnt was to wipe the scones with a wet towel just before they were dipped into the hot fat to keep the surface nice and smooth.

The final step was to display the meat beside the carefully made scone tower with the sweets and treats. This was usually the back of a sheep with its tail still on, grilled or steamed carefully without twisting it. It seemed that the bigger and fattier the tail, the better the quality. The meat was cooked a couple of days before Tsagaan Sar, ready for the big day.

The eve of Tsagaan Sar was always the busiest day of the year. My dad would vacuum the floor and rugs of the whole *ger*, including the space between the supporting poles and the carpets. My mum would be busy dressmaking, sewing one of our new *deels* in a race against time. Zaya and I would be busy dusting, polishing and washing everything we could get our hands on and ironing and folding clothes. We also took the bed covers to the river and dusted them on the fresh snow. Everyone made a great effort to decorate our *ger* beautifully with peacock feathers and china ornaments, and we sewed bright-yellow fringes of fabric with glittery threads all around, just above the curtains. Since the onset of democracy we had not been that bothered about our photos of Lenin or Gagarin – the first cosmonaut – any more, whereas in the time of socialism, having Lenin's photo was a normal thing to do. Some families had his picture beside their Buddhas, referring to him as another 'God'.

Every year on Tsagaan Sar morning we got up very early and prepared the house to perfection before sunrise. It was an incredible feeling, a bit like Christmas Day in the West, I guess. I couldn't sleep, tossing and turning, waiting for the exciting day. My mum would make our first tea of the New Year and sprinkle some of it outside towards the eight sides of the horizon, praying with one hand to her chest in an upright position and one hand holding a shiny new ladle with the tea.

We all put on our best clothes and made an effort to look tidy and stylish. Then, happy with our fine home and ready to welcome guests, we started the day and the New Year. We went around visiting our families, starting with the eldest. When my grandparents and grandfather lived nearby we would start from theirs. We welcomed our relatives, greeting them in the traditional Mongolian way using both hands. The oldest person places his or her arms out straight, with the palms turned down, on the outstretched arms of the youngest person. Each addresses the other with the traditional greeting of good wishes such as: '*Amar sain baina uu? Sar shinedee saikhan shinelej baina uu?*' ('Hello, how do you do? Are you having a nice New Year celebration?') or '*Mend ee, ta saikhan shinelej baina uu?*' ('Hello, are you enjoying yourself at this New Year's celebration?'), while gently touching cheeks. Sometimes they kissed children on their foreheads or cheeks. Others sniffed their heads. Everybody had to greet everyone else apart from husband and wife. We would have queues standing to greet people and then we all sat down. As is tradition, most of the men would swap snuff bottles as a token of friendship and eventually pass them around to the women and the children. We would sniff gently from the half-open snuff bottle before returning it to the owner. These snuff bottles were usually carved out of expensive stone such as granite. Sometimes, as children, we would be naughty and sniff a pinch full of the tobacco from the bottle and have the biggest sneeze ever, almost blowing our heads off. That would leave us with tears streaming from our eyes and running noses, making us look all yucky and funny at the same time.

There is a traditional order, ritual and set of unwritten rules for almost everything at Tsagaan Sar. Once everyone has been greeted, they sit down and are presented with a bowl of tea with milk, salt and a little bit of butter or cream. Then umpteen plates of dumplings are steamed and eaten by the guests. Some families might also prepare potato salads. My mum was good at presenting food beautifully. She would decorate the plateful of dumplings with cabbage leaves and thin slices of beef fat. The people who are considered to be important and particularly the elderly are given the fattiest food as it is considered to be the best. We also had rice with raisins, butter and sugar. I love that food. I could eat bowls and bowls of it. Of course, everyone needs to be aware that they should also leave space for later, as all day and every day of Tsagaan Sar month we eat and drink the same food in different families taking turns. My parents were the oldest among their siblings. So we had most of our visitors on Tsagaan Sar's day – reaching over a hundred people including children some years. At the end of every visit we would each be given a present. My mum would keep a big suitcase behind the curtain on their bed and give out presents for Zaya and I to hand over to the appropriate guests. The women's presents are wrapped in newspapers with a pack of sweets complimenting their main presents. If the relatives are closer to us then the presents are bigger, such as a 4-metre length of silk, enough to make a *deel* or a man's shirt. The children used to receive a handful of sweets, raisins or rare treats like an apple or a mandarin with a pair of tights or notes of a few tugriks.

In the past, Zaya and I have had new jumpers, skirts and jackets as well as sweets. Some families gave us money, which we always handed over to my parents. Having pocket money or simply having some money for ourselves was not an option. We never questioned it and just handed it over.

Some families gave out pencils, pens or notebooks. Even my family had those things, as groups of children kept coming into the *ger* even after dark with their torches in their hands, going around every family in the village, with their routes planned, street by street. When they came they had a sweet from the tall tower of treats and ate some dumplings, then took their presents and left. Most of the time, they were interested only in the presents, so their visits were short. When they came in, my parents would try to guess whose children they were by looking at them, then asking. It was funny that children would soon know which family had better presents and make sure that they visited that family. Mum loved giving out sweets, filling children's hands with treats while my dad checked them out, commenting on their cool hats or *deels*, teasing the children and making them burst into laughter, hiding behind each other.

Tsagaan Sar was a happy period, a chance for extended families to spend time together, but it fell at the coldest part of the year. As well as enjoying the festivities, people naturally used to get colds and coughs during the winter. When I was young, Western medicines were not as readily available as they are now, and we often relied on traditional folk remedies. One of the medicines I grew up drinking was my mum's urine. My parents would encourage us to take it with our eyes closed and in one go. I guess that was the way they did it when they were kids. The salty, savoury taste raced down my throat causing a gagging reflex. Mum used to have a sweet ready as soon as we had finished the urine to get rid of the taste. Mum's urine was also used for reducing a fever.

My parents would dip some cloths in the urine and put them under my arms. The older I got the less my parents used urine and the more they turned to Western medicine.

●

Life changed dramatically for us in 1994, when tragedy struck my father's family once again. Uncle Gana's wife Dash died in a motorbike accident in Sant. The rumour was that she had sat at the back of a motorbike with no helmet and nothing to protect her on a country road. There were three people on the motorbike, and she was right at the back of the pillion. When the bike stalled going up a sandy hill, my aunt rolled off onto the ground and suffered internal bleeding. After the death of her husband, she now died leaving the poor children parentless. My little cousins had lost their young parents just a year apart and now faced being separated from one another. The relatives of both parents decided the children would join a different uncle's or aunt's family individually. The youngest, Dava, was only five. He was a very lively boy and, being the youngest, was spoilt rotten. His sister was only a couple of years older than he was. My mum still tells the story of how she was crying and saying to her little brother, 'You live with Agaa's [my dad's] family. They are the best.' My poor little cousin was making the decision for her younger brother to live with us as she knew my family would provide a good home for him to grow up in, secure and with no lack of food or clothes. So Dava became our little brother. Our little brother with big brown eyes that melted anyone's heart. He was treated the same as we were, although the poor thing obviously missed his mum and dad dearly. Dava was a great help and he was good company. The three of us were always doing things together, and Zaya and Dava became the best of brothers and sisters.

For me, it was also momentous because the year that Dava came to live with us was also the year that I actually moved away from home to study at university in Ulaanbaatar. After years of dreaming about going to this legendary capital city, it was finally time to see it for myself and find out what life-changing opportunities would present themselves.

NINE

First and last Christmas

Believe nothing, no matter where you read it,
or who said it, no matter if I have said it,
unless it agrees with your own reason
and your own common sense.

Buddha

CHRISTMAS TIME, 2009, SCOTLAND. 'What are you talking about, saying my gorgeous boy has a syndrome?! He is a perfect boy!' my mum announced in Mongolian, half talking to herself, and half wishing to reassure us while cuddling and kissing Billy on her lap. Billy looked happy and content, enjoying his granny's attention. I wished it were true. I would have given my arms and legs for Billy not to have Down's syndrome. Richard and I had already accepted as much as we could about Billy's condition.

The atmosphere at home was tense. Having Billy home was in many ways a lovely time, but accepting the extra implications of caring for a child with Down's syndrome was emotionally harsh for all of us. Richard was most worried about Billy's long-term future, together with the ongoing impact on Sara and Simon, who were having to adapt to their brother's disability while learning how to deal with other people's attitudes. There was one time a three-year-old boy, a friend of Simon's, was scared of Billy because of his tubes. Simon was saying, 'He is my baby brother Billy, he is OK,' trying to comfort his friend.

I was in the middle of it all, having to cope with Billy's medical appointments, feed him the right amount and give him his medicine on time. The hardest and the most suffocating thing for me was making my mother properly understand what Down's syndrome was. I think Mum actually understood much of it, but she was just not ready to accept it at all. I could tell Mum and Dad were desperately trying to understand it all and see why Richard and I were so worried about Billy when, in fact, Billy appeared to be so perfect. I was trying to find a way to explain about Down's syndrome but just could not find the right words.

Then one day my parents found a Russian website and they read it together, comparing the symptoms on the site with Billy. It felt like a breakthrough. They then came across a Mongolian website explaining the basic background facts and everything I had wanted to tell them. I was so glad that these websites existed. It meant that my parents could start to understand why Richard and I were anxious about Billy's health. The Mongolian website was started and run by the Mongolian Down's Syndrome Association, which was founded by a woman called Oyun Sanjaasuren, a member of the Mongolian parliament. Oyun is a respected and educated woman in Mongolia. Her oldest son has Down's syndrome and she started the Down's Syndrome Association of Mongolia with a few other parents. There were pictures on the site of Mongolian children with Down's syndrome and their families, doing different activities. I was finally relieved that now my parents knew about Billy's health condition, but I also knew it was still a big issue in Mongolia and in any country to have a child with a disability. My parents started to remember children in Zavhan who might possibly have Down's syndrome. They then realised that it could happen to anyone. Prior to that, in their opinion and in many other people's opinion, disability was usually seen as either a result of something bad that the parents had done, the mistakes of underskilled medical workers, or possibly a hereditary throwback. Looking at both of my parents' relatives, I could not point out anyone with Down's syndrome. It might possibly have helped them if they had known someone with it.

My heart would sink hearing my mother on the phone to her brothers and sisters in Mongolia, who were enquiring after Billy. I knew my parents had told them about Billy's hole in the heart, but not about the Down's syndrome. Perhaps I was being too touchy myself and concentrating too much on 'Down's syndrome' as a term. I was still getting used to accepting our shift in normality myself.

One day we all went out for lunch in a local restaurant. People were looking at Billy and smiling. An elderly woman commented, 'Oh, he is so perfect!' I was pleased that she had said that but inside I was secretly thinking, 'If only you knew he has Down's syndrome and a hole in the heart.' That was the thing with Billy. We could easily have thought of him as a 'normal' baby if the blood test hadn't confirmed that he had that extra chromosome, Trisomy 21. People could not really tell that Billy had Down's syndrome just by looking at him, as the characteristic features were not obvious. I think it had affected Billy more internally than externally.

Christmas day arrived and we celebrated as well as we could for Sara and Simon's sake. It was Billy's first Christmas, and, as visitors from Mongolia, it was also a first experience of Christmas for my parents. For the previous eight years Richard and I had spent Christmas with Margaret, my mother-in-law, either at her home or ours. We had cooked for his mum every year as she was in a wheelchair after suffering a stroke a few years before I met her. Unfortunately, I hadn't met Richard's dad, who had passed away a year before we got together. This year, we celebrated with my parents at home, then took the kids to see their Scottish granny in her nursing home. Richard walked back on his own again later to be with his mum. We thought it could possibly be her last Christmas with us.

After Christmas, around 10th January 2010, we were advised to start feeding Billy through a tube again as his heart had started to struggle. So Richard and I took Billy to hospital and they put the feeding tube into his nose. While waiting for Billy to be intubated, Richard and I had a talk about the future. Well, not really a talk. It was mainly me prodding him to speak. Richard had been so taciturn since Billy's diagnosis, and I would have to ask pointed questions and goad him in many ways just to get some words out of him. I wanted to know what he was thinking, and how he was feeling emotionally. I found it frustrating when he fell silent with his arms folded, hiding behind an unemotional detached mask, saying nothing.

Then we were disturbed by one of the nurses, who walked into the room with Billy in her arms. He looked blue and lifeless. I started to cry. The nurse took Billy back to get him checked over again. She said he had turned blue when they put the tube up his nose. After an hour or so it was decided that I should stay with Billy in the hospital overnight to learn how to feed him through the tube. There was some kind of viral outbreak among young children in the ward, so Billy and I were kept in the corner room away from the others. We were discharged home the next day.

●

A few days later, Billy had to be admitted to hospital again as he needed oxygen. Mary, our health visitor, had come in for her routine check-up and had immediately noticed how blue Billy was. I felt bad that we hadn't noticed his colour. His complexion was normally slightly bluer because of his heart defect, so the deterioration in colour had come on gradually rather than suddenly. Mary phoned the doctor, who saw us that afternoon. Billy was sent back to the same ward to be on oxygen. I couldn't stay with him, though: Richard had to work and I had to be home for Simon and Sara, especially as Sara had badly scalded her left thigh with boiling tea by accident a few days earlier. I had made three cups of tea and took two through to the living room for my parents. By the time I was about to come back for the third cup, Sara was trying to help by loading the dishwasher and, thinking that the cup of tea was empty, she had knocked it over herself. She screamed with a high-pitched voice and we all came running to see what had happened. I grabbed the phone and dialled 999 while pouring cold water on her leg. My parents were holding Billy and keeping Simon away from the kitchen. The ambulance came and I went to the hospital with Sara, leaving the boys with their grandparents. A few hours later Richard brought Sara and I home from the hospital with some dressing supplies.

I was now the one changing Sara's dressings and she had to stay in bed most of the time. She was back and forward to the hospital, being checked regularly in the ward next to where Billy was. So I would take Simon and Sara to hospital, and visit Billy at the same time. The children's wards were getting to know us. Every day, I would arrive at the hospital, pushing Simon and Sara in a hospital wheelchair. I would check how Billy's oxygen level had been and give him a bath and change his clothes.

A few days later it was time for my parents to go back to Mongolia. They had been with us for about two months.

On 15th January 2010, I drove my parents to Glasgow Airport at about 4am. I sobbed in the car after seeing them off. I cried not because I was going to miss my parents; I cried because I had this tremendous urge to protect Billy. He was the one uppermost in my mind as he needed the most attention and care at that moment. He was the youngest, he was the baby of the family, he was the disabled one, he was the sick one who needed most attention. I was upset that I couldn't be beside him in hospital, cuddling him and bonding with him properly. On my way back from the airport on that dark January morning I went to see Billy. I couldn't drive near the hospital without making a ten-minute diversion to call in. I managed to enter the hospital through the night entrance where there was a security system in place. My tiny baby boy was asleep with his face full of plasters holding his oxygen tube and his feeding tube. It was so good to see him every time. That was where his mummy was supposed to be, beside her baby.

I checked the notes to see how many times he had been fed and changed. All seemed normal. Then I was on my way home before the others were up. Is this going to be our new normal? How is Billy going to survive? I need to sleep. So tired.

TEN

Open your eyes,
open your eyes

Treat a person as he is, and he will remain as he is.
Treat him as he could be, and he will
become what he should be.

American football coach Jimmy Johnson

AUGUST 1994. After a four-day drive over 1,000km of rough terrain from Sant to Ulaanbaatar, I arrived in the capital thanks to a relative and his family with their glossy jeep. I remember other families regularly taking their children with them when they went back and forth to the capital city, while I waited patiently for my turn. I was always told that I would finally get there when I went to university, and now here I was. My mother, excited herself and not a little proud that I was at last getting to see the city I had only dreamt of, came along to help me sort out my accommodation and university enrolment.

Despite the fact that it was the end of August and a tor-rential downpour over the previous few days had virtually destroyed the rudimentary country road, the journey to Ulaanbaatar was easier if longer than the ones I had been used to during my last two years studying in Uliastai, away from my family in Sant. Then, desperate to see my parents for two weeks during the school holidays, we would travel on top of a frozen meat and salt truck in the extreme cold of 30°C or sometimes even lower. We kept warm by snug-gling up to each other in our sheepskin *deels*, felt boots and furry hats. Compared with that, I was in clover for the journey to Ulaanbaatar, comfortably settled in the front passenger seat of a shiny new jeep, travelling in an August temperature of about 10°C. We would casually drive for a few hours each day, then stop at any convenient river or lake, where we swam and had some noodles with lamb, which we'd prepared earlier, in our tea, heated on a mod-ern gas camping cooker, before spending the nights in tents my family had brought with us. Our companions were my mother's fourth- or fifth-generation relatives, a family net-work I couldn't really get my head around properly when my mum explained it to me. It seemed that my mother's grandmother was related to their grandmother. But, hey, it's always handy to have a relative who can give you a cross-country lift. They lived in Ulaanbaatar and were returning with their two girls, aged 8 and 12, after a summer holiday in the countryside.

We approached the city after sunset, and I was struck by the car lights, which looked like stars at night, but with one line of white and the other one red. I had never seen so many cars before and, with the city lighting up the night sky, I noticed people wearing light-coloured clothes, mostly white T-shirts and dresses. I thought it must be clean here if you can wear that all day. In the countryside, when you are looking after sheep and goats, you can't really wear such clothes without getting them dirty and dusty.

That evening we were dropped off at my uncle Baabaa's in one of the Soviet-style blocks of flats, each nine storeys high and with names like 'Happiness' and 'Friendship'. Uncle Baabaa's apartment was on the fourth floor of the Happiness building, where he lived with his wife and daughter, who is two years younger than I am. I marvelled at everything in Ulaanbaatar; there's so much to see and do in this place, I thought. The next day I 'practised' buying a carton of milk on my own. The entrance and stairwell were a bit complicated, designed in a pentagon shape with no windows, and if the lights were out it was like negotiating a blacked-out maze just to get to street level. Mum was pleased when I found my way back without getting lost.

It had been arranged that I would live with them for my first year at university. My uncle was a minister in the government and was always very busy. My aunt cooked delicious meals with different vegetables that I had never seen before. My cousin Enkhe was a city girl with her 'white' complexion. Before I arrived, she had her own room, which I was now to share, and we agreed to have our own sides. I have to say I was a bit of an embarrassment to her around her friends. My self-confidence was low, and I felt conscious of my tanned skin and long, tightly plaited pigtails beside these fair-skinned, streetwise city girls.

My uncle gave me a tour of the flat, including the bathroom and toilet. He showed me how to flush the toilet and then moved onto the bathroom. 'You shouldn't sit down in the bath. You are a girl. It's better if you stand and have a shower,' he advised. I wondered why I couldn't sit down and had my first shower standing, but it was a great feeling to have a room to wash myself. I hardly remembered a time when I'd had nothing on. The door was locked and I was singing with freedom, noticing every detail in the bathroom. I enjoyed that shower. Ever since I was little I had mostly used a metal basin to wash my hair and then my legs at home. In the summer we used to swim in the local river: Bogdiin Gol ('Bogd River') in Uliastai, and Holboo Nuur ('Twin Lakes') in Sant.

My uncle was excited for me too, showing me round the city for the first time. He took me and Mum out for a walk after dinner, when it was getting dark but was still warm. A gentle breeze played with my long hair and I was walking between Baabaa and my mum, filled with excitement. Baabaa said, 'Let's go in here,' leading us to a shop with a colourful neon sign saying 'Paradox'. He bought me a red can of something and handed it to me. Filled with anticipation, I tasted it. Baabaa and my mum were both looking at me waiting for my response. I liked it. It was Coca-Cola. So at 17 I tasted a can of Coke for the first time. My journey was beginning. I was no longer a little schoolgirl and people were now taking me seriously. Wonderful.

I started my first year at The Institute of Foreign Languages, which during the socialist time was called the Russian Language Pedagogical Institute. But by the time I started, it was possible to study other languages and I enrolled for English and Russian, which meant that English was the main language. I enjoyed being a student, making new friends from all over Mongolia and working with teachers from around the world. We had teachers from Britain through VSO and American teachers through the Peace Corps. We also had a Korean teaching us English. I think he was there through some kind of Christian religious background, thanks mainly to his wife's involvement. His methods were old-fashioned compared to the other teachers. We would repeat the words loudly together again and again as a group. Although he was seen as strict he came across as a warm and caring person.

Some teachers were better than others. We had a lovely American teacher called Kathy from Colorado who taught us with all her heart. She would dress casually in long, flowery skirts and was fun to have as a teacher. She was modest and patient with us, unlike one of the male teachers called Ron. Ron was married to a Japanese woman and he had a very snobbish attitude towards us. He would take off his watch from his wrist and show off that it was a designer brand. When he lost his temper in the classroom he would shout at students very close to their faces; consequently, there was a negative atmosphere every time he taught us. So we complained to the English department and his manner was found to be unprofessional in every class he taught. The university sacked him based on students' feedback.

Shirley, from Chicago, was our strictest teacher and good at making us learn English grammar thoroughly. She would occasionally invite a couple of students to her flat for dinner, and I went there a couple of times with other students. She lived in a block where most foreigners lived near the Sansar tunnel. Her way of living was very different from ours. For one thing, she had a security-code entry system at the door; and once inside her apartment, stylishly decorated with floor lamps and plants on the windowsills, we could have been anywhere in the world. This was to be my first experience of using a knife and a fork with a napkin on my knees. It was so bizarre and an amazing experience – everything felt different and new. The floor lamp standing in the corner lit the room elegantly and she cooked a meal following a recipe, something else I had never seen before since we always knew what and how to cook our Mongolian dishes.

I shared my dream with Shirley over the dinner table: 'I want to go to America or England after university and do a Masters.' She was quick with an answer, and, I guess, just being realistic. 'You can't, you need money. It's also very expensive to live there.' I was disheartened. I felt as if she had said, 'You would never be able to do that.' The comment made me want to travel the world even more, but for now I just wanted to do well in my studies.

My other favourite teacher was David, who was in his 50s. He was from England and lectured in English Literature. It was fun going to his classes and I never missed any of his lectures. He had taught in England, where he eventually became a university lecturer. He would jump up and down and act out the speeches from books, his voice rising and falling and his eyes changing according to the character. He had moved to Mongolia with his wife a few years earlier, mainly because his wife was involved in charity works and the Baha'i faith.

Some of my teachers were Mongolians who had travelled the world and seen a lot; most of them had postgraduate degrees and doctorates from English-speaking countries that were in one way or another important to Mongolian society. The head of the English department took our class a few times; she was a petite woman in her late 40s who always looked perfect, with her carefully done hair and make-up. She walked taller than she was, wearing high heels and holding her head high. In one particular lesson, she was disappointed when she showed us a photo of a woman I did not recognise. I did not have a clue; I was looking stupid and feeling bad that I could not answer this important woman's question. The head's eyes widened and her face fell. She sighed and pointed to the photo and declared, 'This is Madonna. Open your eyes. Open ... your ... eyes!' fluttering her eyelashes quickly with her hands opening and closing near her eyes. That funny image reduced us to giggles. After that, if any of us didn't know something we would do the same to each other and end up in laughter.

●

When democracy began to develop, Mongolia opened up to all kinds of different religious influences, and many of us went to these new churches and meetings to improve our English. I attended meetings in Christian churches with no knowledge of the differences between them. I also spent time exploring the Baha'i faith, and I enjoyed these meetings more than some of the others because we were encouraged to discuss and communicate with each other on different topics and nobody was judgemental.

I went a few times to a Christian sect run by some South Koreans, who started by teaching us the Adam and Eve story. Then, gradually, young female Mongolian students started being paired up with handsome men in South Korea. We never saw the men, but we were shown some photos of handsome candidates who looked like models. We were told we were lucky to be chosen and matched, as not many people were good enough for these arrangements. As soon as this happened to one of my friends, I stopped going because I just could not believe that someone could be your husband before you had even met him. I was not that easily sucked into something I didn't believe in, though some of my friends still went, aspiring to be the next lucky one to leave Mongolia and marry their heaven-sent husbands in South Korea. Later I heard that members of the Unification Church, often referred to as the *Moonies*, were active in Mongolia.

My parents reminded me that I was a country girl there in Ulaanbaatar to study – not to waste my time. As I'm the oldest I had a future responsibility to look after my sister

Zaya and, now, my brother Dava. I was always small and slim and I still wore my long hair in pigtails, which sometimes caused confusion, with some teachers asking me what I was doing at university. I would sit in the front row in every lecture, trying not to miss anything they said. So, before every exam time, my notebooks would do the rounds of the students' rooms. Some of my classmates would borrow and photocopy my lecture notes while others copied them by hand, day and night. No wonder examiners were sometimes confused when several of us had the same answers. I didn't think of it until the lecturer of Mongolian Literature threw my homework notebook across the room in a fury. He was questioning us in alphabetical order, so my name was near the end. In his eyes, I had the same answers as many of my classmates. Of course he didn't believe it when I told him I was the one who went to the library and did the homework. I learnt my lesson after that. I was trying hard to do well, not just for myself but for my parents. I wanted them to feel proud as they have always done so much for me.

My parents paid my university fees by selling hand-combed cashmere from our own goats. Every autumn for four years after the summer holidays I came back to Ulaanbaatar by car accompanied by 80kg of goat cashmere in three or four big cotton sacks. These I would take to the raw material market in Ulaanbaatar and sell to the open-air traders there. My parents showed us how to pick out the unwanted dirt and coarse hair by hand to make it look better quality and thus get a better price. The price for a kilo of cashmere reached its peak and we sold our cashmere for 40 thousand tugriks, which was then around £20 a kilo.

It would have been very easy to lose focus living away from my parents and with money in my hands. Some students partied nonstop until they ran out of money, whereas others could not get out of bed as they had been blinded by love. One of my closest friends dropped out of college as she preferred going to the cinema and eating out, having great fun. Her parents were not told about it until two years later. Luckily for her, she was from a well-off family who could afford that financially, unlike mine. I did not dare to drink alcohol or let my hair down too much, constantly aware as I was of my parents' hard work and love for me.

●

In my second year at university I started living in a student dormitory, sharing a room with four other girls in my class. The five of us were from different provinces all around Mongolia and we got on well, sharing everything we had. Our age range was between 18 and 24. I was the youngest and Baska Egch was the eldest. We called her *egch* meaning 'sister'. In Mongolia, people often call other people 'sister', 'brother', 'uncle', 'aunt', 'granny' and 'grandpa'. It's a respect thing. I would talk about Zaya as my sister, and I would also talk about my aunt as my sister. No wonder Westerners would get confused when I told them I had one sister and then she seems to be working as a midwife, ophthalmologist, tax officer and student. In Mongolia, people call their mother-in-law 'mum' too. So people would end up having two mothers and two fathers. My parents distinguished my two grandfathers as the tall father and the short father. Unfortunately, I knew only one grandmother as my maternal grandmother had passed away when I was only one.

Amaraa was the singer in our room. In fact, she represented the university in a student song contest in Ulaanbaatar, singing Whitney Houston songs beautifully. I had never heard of Whitney Houston until then. When we went to see Amaraa at a contest we cheered and made as much supporting noise as we could. Then one of us would wrap the artificial flowers we used to decorate our room in colourful paper and present them to Amaraa when she had finished her song. Over three evenings we went to see her singing different songs, and the same flowers were wrapped in three different colours of paper, with us taking turns to go on the stage and give her the flowers and a kiss. Being students, we didn't have much money and it worked well as Amaraa would return home with the flowers each night. We would have such a laugh, walking home arm in arm, commenting on how popular Amaraa was with her flower-giving fans. We threw a party when Amaraa won the contest with Houston's song 'I Will Always Love You'.

During my time as a student my parents always sent me meat for the winter from our livestock. Every October and November throughout the country there is a huge slaughtering of sheep, goats, cows, horses and sometimes camels, when people choose the weaker animals that might not survive the harsh Mongolian winter. The winter is so cold in Mongolia that the meat is kept outside, where it stays frozen until springtime. A deep-freeze is -18°C, but Mongolian winters are colder, reaching -50°C in some places. It is also the time when we dry the meat for the next summer. It is thinly sliced and put on a line like washing inside the sheds. Months go by and the meat is then ready to be stored in cotton sacks for use in the summer.

Nomadic families move around the countryside following the best grass for their livestock during the four seasons. There is no guarantee of electricity wherever they move, so they don't rely on fridges and freezers. Having the dried meat *borts* helps to keep things simple. It can be eaten even in tea and it is delicious. My mum was not well for much of my childhood and we would bring the freshest water from the spring and eat the freshest meat we could. So during the summer time, having no fridge in the countryside, we dried meat outside in the sun, smoking it with cow dung. The smoke kept flies away as well as preserving the meat, and it made it taste delicious.

At one point in my third year, I had no money left apart from my 20 thousand tugriks (then about £10), which I didn't want to touch unless absolutely necessary. That year I shared a room with two other friends. I found two empty bottles of juice, took 100 tugriks from my own 20 thousand and bought two bottles of fizzy orange juice from a nearby juice factory. Because I took my own bottles, the juice was reduced to half price. I put a notice on our room door saying 'Juice for sale here.' I sold the two bottles and went to buy four more with the money and so on. To make more money I also bought some scones and biscuits from a relative's bakery and sold them from my room. Students were buying my juice and scones, and it meant that I was making enough money to buy my own food. At times, I went to the big open-air market at weekends early in the morning and bought jars of cucumber at wholesale prices, then sold them individually throughout the day. I enjoyed making money; I felt a sense of achievement that I did not need someone to come and rescue me. I did not have to rely on anybody.

I also gave private lessons in English and Mongolian. I was lucky to be selected to do my teaching practice in a private university for a month. After it had finished they offered me a part-time job teaching English to first- and second-year students, even though I wasn't fully qualified at the time. I couldn't believe how lucky I was. I tried not to take money from my parents when I was a student. I remember going to a parliamentary election campaign where the candidate talked about students working in the Western world. He had worked in a restaurant as a waiter when he studied in England. It was the first time I'd heard that students working and earning money was considered normal. In Mongolia, parents supply everything until their children get married. They prepare their children's home, including the furniture. In the western part of Mongolia, where I'm from, the groom's family prepares the *ger* and all of the furniture apart from the bed and the chest of drawers, which the bride brings with her on the wedding day.

In the summer holidays, when most of my classmates stayed in Ulaanbaatar working as tour guides in order to practise their English, I always went home to Sant. My parents expected me to come back and help out with the sheep and goats, and I used to take a book and a dictionary with me while I was looking after our livestock, inwardly annoyed with my parents but unable to say it to their faces. Instead, I'd mutter to myself, 'My friends are speaking English with tourists and I'm speaking baa baa with sheep.' My parents must have picked up on the fact that I was not happy at times. They would say, 'In winter, you do brain work. In summer, it's good to do manual work. It's good for your brain.'

Of course, I loved being at home with my parents, Zaya and Dava, and not worrying about money or food; I was like a dependent child again. The days went quickly, and our daily routine went like this: milking the cows, cleaning the *ger*, collecting dung, making yogurt, cheese, curds, vodka and butter while enjoying the beautiful scenery – with moonlight at night and the streaming sunlight during the day.

Sometimes, boys around my age would drop by on horseback in groups of three or four. There is a saying in Mongolian for these kinds of visits: 'Checking out whose girls have grown beautifully and whose *airag* (mare's milk) has fermented well.' I never particularly liked that saying. It made me feel as if we girls were on display and these people were on a shopping spree to see who was available. I know some families tell their boys to go and make friends with specific girls from certain families because of their family history. The families were assessed according to financial status, work status, health history and reputation in the community.

In Zavhan tradition, first the groom's family sends a messenger to inform the bride's family of the groom's intentions with regard to an engagement ceremony, although some families would decide who their sons should go for anyway. The engagement ceremony is done in a traditional way a few weeks after the announcement. The bride's family then decide if they want to give their daughter away to that family, by way of their son. If they agree, they sniff the snuff bottle offered to them by the visitor from the groom's family. If they don't want their daughter to be married to the guy, they turn down the snuff bottle without sniffing it. Sometimes, the bride's family demands that the groom's family does the ceremony three times, then they sniff the bottle on the third time. On very rare occasions, the bride's family sniffs the snuff bottle from another family because they prefer the son of that family. Many girls marry very young, at just 16, as soon as they finish school. Who would've thought it would be my turn to be considered as a bride soon?

ELEVEN

To be or not to be

It is easier to build strong children than to repair broken men.

Frederick Douglass

WHEN I GRADUATED from university in 1998 I was 21 and I was expecting Sara. In fact, three of us were pregnant that year in my university class. We all lived in the student dormitory and we all had student boyfriends. I had known my then boyfriend since we were in kindergarten in Uliastai, but we didn't go out together until the second year of my time at university. He lived and studied in a different city so we saw each other only once a month or so. When I graduated he still had a year of his studies to finish and I went back to Sant, which meant it was impossible to see each other at all for a year as the distance was over 1,000km.

Earlier that year, on a beautiful summer morning, a relative of my boyfriend had pulled up on a white horse outside our *ger* in Bayan Nuur. He looked very smart, dressed in a brown silk *deel* with every button done up, even wearing a dressy hat. He lived in Bayan Ulaan, which meant that it was out of his way just to drop by. He was self-conscious and trying awkwardly to make conversation with my parents. They were teasing him as they were old schoolmates, asking where he was heading looking so smart. He replied, 'I came to let you know that you will have proposal guests in a few weeks for your older daughter.'

I was in the small spare *ger* cooking with Zaya and Dava. My mum came in and whispered into my ear, 'He came to let us know that you are to be engaged.' I was surprised as I didn't think my boyfriend's family, who lived in Uliastai, would send someone to deliver the message because my boyfriend's father was a widower and I wasn't sure he would be aware of such customs. I was 21 and, at the time, some of my classmates from school had been already married for a few years. In many people's eyes I was the right age to get married and start a family.

Three weeks later, on the night before the engagement ceremony, my paternal grandfather, my dad's uncle Nainaa and a couple of my uncles came from Uliastai in a jeep. My dad had phoned them to let them know about the ceremony. On the morning of the ceremony, my maternal uncles came with their wives and children.

Soon the proposal guests arrived on two white horses. They greeted my family, who sat in our *ger*, filling the right side. In keeping with tradition, my boyfriend was not there and neither was I. I kept myself away from it all, cooking in the spare *ger* while sending Zaya and Dava to eavesdrop. I was petrified, not knowing what they were going to say or do. Everyone was wearing their silk *deels* apart from the three of us cooking and making tea for people. About three hours later the guests offered their snuff bottle to my parents. First my dad was given the bottle in his right hand. Then my mum, and then everyone else, from my grandfather to my youngest uncle, all sniffed the bottle, agreeing that they were happy for us to get married. They decided that we had already found each other and they had no need to object to our wishes. I was glad it was over.

●

Not long after the engagement it was autumn. We moved back to our pink house in Sant centre, to spend the winter in our *ger* as the baby would need a warmer home. My boyfriend was away studying for his final year. My family and I erected the *ger* in a fenced yard near the pink house, which was particularly handy, being just five minutes' walk from the hospital.

My parents encouraged me to keep active while preparing to give birth. I would wash the floor sitting down and gather dung as much as I could during the day, walking long distances in the fresh air, hauling water from the river. The biggest job that Zaya, Dava and I did that autumn was sawing up a truckful of logs by hand. We then chopped the wood into small pieces for winter fuel. It was a nice feeling to spend time with my sister and brother, singing and having a laugh, telling jokes and getting hysterical at each other's sense of humour. The work seemed more fun than a chore. We were amazed at how well we did it. My parents were proud of us as every year previously they had hired people to do it with an electric saw.

Nearer the baby's due date, Mum's sister, my aunt Duuluu, came from Uliastai to help deliver my baby. My parents had arranged all this and I had no idea what was expected. Duuluu is an experienced midwife in Uliastai and is well known for her good reputation. She has received medals for her record of attending over ten thousand babies' births in the province. She brought me a book on pregnancy and birth. I found it scary and fascinating to read about unborn babies and examine the diagrams and pictures. I guess it was a last chance for me to read up on everything, but I knew there were people in the countryside who give birth without the need for any books. Zaya would sneak outside, hiding behind the *ger* to read the book with great interest. She was fourteen that year. I pretended I didn't know this, allowing her to save face. I knew what it was like to be a teenager. I used to do the same with one of my parents' books, *Before and After Marriage*.

I was getting fed up with myself, and with other people asking when the baby was coming. Then one night it all started while Duuluu was away visiting her in-laws. I couldn't settle to sleep and the feeling got worse as time went by. At about 5 o'clock in the morning my parents got up and kindled the fire and my mum lit a self-made candle in front of the Buddha and the picture of my late grandparents, praying for all to go well.

Then Mum offered me her warm urine to drink, saying, 'This'll help. This is good for you. That's what I did when I had you.' She gave me one of her hidden treats in the locked chest: 'Have a sweet.' I couldn't keep anything down at that stage; it all came up quicker than it went down. Luckily, Duuluu came back and she told me to walk around outside, so I walked for a bit. But I was in so much pain that I then asked my dad to press on my back as I crawled about inside the *ger*. Duuluu was basically telling me to do things to distract me. She said, 'Hold the bed frame and that will help.' Oh boy, I had never experienced this kind of pain, and I was almost at my wits' end. My poor parents were running around me offering things and Duuluu was checking me to see if I was ready to go to hospital. Finally, it was time to make the five-minute walk to hospital, which I did with my parents on each side holding my hands. I was like a toddler between contractions, taking a few steps and then having to stop. We finally managed to get into the hospital, which had no heating and no electricity. It was the end of September, but not yet the date that the central heating was to be fired up. There were only two or three days until October – the 1st of October was the day it was to be switched on in Sant. The school, the hospital and the offices all got their heating from the same source: hot water pumped from the local solid-fuel power station through a network of huge, lagged pipes.

As we walked into the hospital, I was directed to the labour room by one of the two staff working that day. I didn't realise how noisy I had become until the nurse said, 'Oh my! You are a loud one, aren't you?!' I was embarrassed. I thought to myself, I will not let you see how noisy I am. I was worried she would tell people how loud I was and that everyone would talk about me in Sant. What nonsense! At least that comment helped me to control myself. I was behaving very well now. Duuluu was allowed to come and help deliver the baby. She was praising me, 'Look how good my niece is. She doesn't cry.' I was thinking to myself why would I cry? I just need to get my baby out.

A couple of hours later, at about 1pm, my baby girl was born. Sara looked around as if she was checking out this big wide world. Duuluu examined Sara and said, 'She's a healthy baby girl!' Then she wrapped her in the blanket my mum had made and whisked her out of the room to show to my parents, who were waiting outside the room.

After bonding with Sara on my chest, we were taken into the only room in the maternity ward of the hospital. There was one other mother there with her baby girl. In a heartbeat, my life ceased to be just mine any more as I observed my darling daughter in my arms as she looked for food and warmth. I was overwhelmed with the rush of love and protectiveness for this little person and I then realised my parents' love for me. Yeah, I am a lucky person to have parents like mine, but now it's my turn to care for my baby and give her the love she will need. I had a shaky, insecure feeling inside about my fiancé, as I wasn't sure if we had what it takes to be a strong couple. We didn't have a strong future plan, apart from being engaged in the traditional way. But for now, I was doing the best I could for my daughter...

TWELVE

Sheep or city

I dream my painting and I paint my dream.
Vincent van Gogh

'DON'T LOOK BACK NOW, just run to the car!' My dad hurried me towards his work jeep parked on the other side of the river. He had asked his colleague to give me a lift to Sant centre. It was early August, so our *ger* was on the bank of the river Hungui, where we were looking after our animals for the summer. Sara was only eight months old and she was howling and crying her eyes out, as if she knew I was going away and leaving her. She was trying to get hold of my dress when I passed her, grabbing at my bag on the way out. I had a quick look around to see how she was. My baby girl was desperately trying to come to her mummy with her hands reaching forward in an attempt to crawl towards me. I felt like going back and picking her up to comfort her, saying, 'Mummy isn't going anywhere.'

But I rushed away, hearing my parents telling me not to look back and just go. Crossing the river on foot, I ran to get into the waiting jeep. I knew why my parents were telling me to do it. They were trying to make me strong and not dwell on missing my baby. They were worried I might not go. They thought I would waste my degree in teaching English and Russian in a small rural area, forgetting what I had already learnt, and would be in danger of being stuck in my career and life. Once we reached Sant, I stayed overnight in our pink building in the village centre, then I climbed into another jeep, which was heading to Ulaanbaatar. I was still breastfeeding then, expressing milk every time we stopped on the way to the city, trying not to think of my baby, pulling myself together, promising my daughter inwardly that 'Mummy will come and get you once I've built a nice home for both of us'.

The year I had spent living with my parents in their *ger* in Sant had gone by so quickly. Every time I fed my baby in my arms and changed her nappies in candlelight during the cold winter nights, I had reflected on my life. I was lucky to have my parents, who would do anything for me. They looked after me and Sara with no expectation of being paid back.

I tried as much as I could to make the most of what I knew and what I could do during this time. I organised and ran an English course for local children and a few adults, making enough money to buy a truck full of logs, thus contributing towards the vital winter fuel. My parents needed more fuel that year precisely because we had a baby. The management in the local authority were keen that I shouldn't leave Sant, so they offered me a position as a secondary school English teacher in return for 500 sheep and goats. The animals would have been more than enough to make a living together with the teaching work, but I turned down the offer and was soon on my way to the capital. I made my mind up about my relationship with my fiancé, too, after I heard that he had been seeing another woman in the city where he lived. I am not the kind of person who continually gives people second chances when it comes to life decisions. All of this was possible only because my parents offered to look after my daughter in Sant until I had found my own feet in Ulaanbaatar.

●

While living in the countryside and thinking things through, I had considered what skills I needed in order to do well in my career. The two most important were learning English and being adept at computer work in the newly democratic Mongolia. As my BA was in teaching English I decided to concentrate on my computing skills. As soon as I came to Ulaanbaatar I started learning how to use a computer, and, in return, I taught English to my computer teacher.

During this period I was working for a small language firm, but I was also looking for a job with a future, one that would help me to continue to improve my English and send me on different courses. At that time, it was hard to know where to find out what jobs were available – there was no organised online system and the newspaper that did have a section for job vacancies in the city had no opportunities I would have liked. The only way then to find out about jobs was by word of mouth.

In that way, I heard from a former classmate at university that there was a teaching opportunity in a State college. I was pleased by the positive response I got throughout the application process and the interview. But, just as they were about to offer me the job after the interview stage, a Mongolian lady in charge noticed that I had stated that I had a child on my application. Her tone changed. She challenged me:

'What happens if your child is sick?'

'She is not here. She is living with my parents. They live a thousand kilometres away from here,' I explained.

111

'Well, we don't know that. What happens if the child falls ill? You would leave your work and look after your child. Then we would have to find someone else to do your job,' the woman snapped at me.

I could see that the other teacher, who was a native English speaker, thought this was unreasonable. But he didn't seem to have the power to overrule the woman. I left without the job, feeling angry and frustrated. I can't hide my baby. She is here and it's my job to look after her. As I left the college, I felt this strong determination to show these people just how well I could do, and so, wiping away my tears, I stomped out, determined to get an even better job than that one.

At the time, I was staying with my uncle Sukhee and aunt Byambaa, who had always been there for me. They wanted me to do well and they cared for me as if I was staying in a hotel. I called my aunt Byambaa 'Ajaa', meaning 'Sister' Byambaa. She had looked after me when I was little and we already had a special bond. She was the first person I would talk to if I had any secrets or problems. Sukhee Ah (Byambaa Ajaa's husband) was good to me, too. They liked having me around to look after their two children in the evenings if they were going out. Sukhee Ah would comment, 'When you are here looking after the little ones, we can go out without worrying about anything.' They weren't so happy to trust some of the other relatives. I guess their kids were used to me and I really loved my cousins. Besides, I was good at cooking and housework when I was around.

Every morning, I would dress as smartly as I could and go off job hunting as the language firm job was only part-time for a limited period. I walked around the streets of Ulaanbaatar, exploring every door with English signs, looking for a better opportunity. Having lived in Sant, which was such a remote rural village, it was all a bit of a culture shock and I worried about my confidence and the way I dressed. I wasn't really aware of how unfashionable I looked with my long hair with no style, and my clothes were neither the right look for the jobs I was going for, or, for that matter, my age. I didn't know what to do with my long hair, so I gelled the top of it back as if I didn't have any hair and had a ponytail at the back. It must have looked ridiculous. My mum had given me her best work suits and skirts, so I was dressed like a forty-something secondary school teacher. My confidence to talk to people had gone and I felt so old-fashioned in the fast-moving city life.

I managed to find a temporary teaching job, which enabled me to rent a bedsit in the city centre and I started, for the first time in my life, living independently. I found a couple of books written by Dale Carnegie, an American guru in self-development and salesmanship. I wrote quotes from Carnegie's book *How to Win Friends and Influence People* around my rented bedsit. My fridge door Post-it would tell me to smile: 'A smile is contagious. Find things to smile about and share your smile with the world.' And the little mirror Post-it instructed me to: 'Give honest, sincere appreciation.' The whole room was covered with Post-its and I worked on one quote a week. I started feeling happier and noticing more positive things in life. I was practising my positive quotes everywhere I went. The outcome was incredible. I was complimenting people sincerely and, in return, people appreciated my kind words. Making others smile made me happy.

Then one day, I got lucky. I was passed a message saying that my university teacher David was asking for me. David was working in a language school then considered to be the best in Mongolia. They had a teaching vacancy and David had thought of me and wondered if I was available and living in Ulaanbaatar. As my tutor, David knew me well. He had observed my teaching practices and was always professional in his feedback. So I phoned the school and spoke to him. He told me the school was desperate for a teacher as the new term was starting in two weeks' time. Then he called me back and asked if I would come in for an interview. I was really excited but extremely nervous.

With my gelled-back hair and much effort to look smart, I turned up at the school and reported to the posh-looking receptionist who seemed to be in charge of just about everything. Soon, the deputy head teacher came out and invited me in. As I entered the room the head teacher was waiting for me. The two women both looked educated and sophisticated, dressed well in their smart suits and high heels. They fired their questions at me in turn. I answered as well as I could from what I knew. After about half an hour, they asked me to wait outside while they discussed it together.

I waited outside impatiently while checking out all the interesting posters in the school corridor. The posters were from Britain, Australia, the United States and New Zealand. The school had a magical feeling to it. Everyone looked confident and satisfied with where they were. There was a little canteen with about six tables and a library at the end of the corridor.

I was daydreaming hopefully about working there when the deputy head called me in and offered me the job. I couldn't believe it! I left the school almost running, so elated that I was hopping and jumping in the street. I was beaming as I ran to the bus stop to go and see Byambaa Ajaa. I did it. I couldn't think of any other employer I would have been happier to be working for. The library was full of glossy printed books instead of the black and white photocopied material

I used in other places. Each teacher had a desk and a little tape recorder instead of teaching in rented locations with no stability. The school was well equipped with DVD players, TVs and even a video camera.

Two weeks later, I was in the classrooms teaching English as a Foreign Language to adults, enjoying every moment of it. As the salary was about 200 thousand tugriks a month, I was earning so much more than in my other job. I was teaching fewer hours but had more money and good support. More money meant that my gelled hair was transformed into something more stylish, and my clothes started to look similar to those of my colleagues who had been there for a while. My confidence improved and I was able to send some sacks of flour and sugar home, as well as little things for my daughter and for my parents.

Thanks to my parents, I was feeling 'young, free and single' after being an impoverished undergraduate with hardly any experience of nightlife during my student years. Now I was meeting up with friends at weekends and was out dancing in nightclubs till the small hours of the morning. There were some foreign colleagues who were happy for me to tag along wherever they were going and I would meet more foreign people and make friends with them, too. Needless to say, growing up in the countryside and not using a knife and fork caused me to feel extremely uncomfortable at first.

My foreign friends took me to Café de France, run by a Corsican whose customers seemed to be mostly foreigners who were missing their homes. The meals seemed to me to consist of the most exotic and bizarre food I had ever seen — it was there that I tried spaghetti Bolognese for the first time. I now had the opportunity to explore different experiences.

I was like a wooden doll, watching everything, listening to many different languages buzzing around me, self-conscious about everything. I would watch others first to see how they picked up their knives and forks, putting their napkins on their laps, pouring wine into their elegant tall glasses before raising them in a toast. It was a surreal experience, a different world from the Mongolia I knew, with an utterly different way of socialising. I couldn't help noticing that many of these people seemed to be rich foreign men, some of them accompanied by young, pretty Mongolian women.

My colleagues earned about the same as I did, so we would go Dutch, but we couldn't afford to go to places like Café de France that often. Ulaanbaatar then was opening itself up to all sorts of businesses and services, and the city was filling up with Western-named bars, hotels and nightclubs such as the Hard Rock and Tornado. The number of tourists was rising each year and Mongolia was changing rapidly. Almost everyone dreamt of going abroad and bringing back money to buy a house and a car. Ulaanbaatar had districts of *gers* as well as grey Soviet-built concrete buildings in rows. Everyone dreamt of having a flat in there, in one of the fashionable areas in Ulaanbaatar.

Anyone who spoke any English was trying to sit English tests like TOEFL (Test Of English as a Foreign Language) or IELTS (International English Language Testing System), mostly in order to study in America, England, Australia or New Zealand. Later on, it seemed that anywhere would do as long as it was abroad. Unfortunately, this policy made many Mongolians vulnerable to crimes such as forgery, human trafficking and illegal deeds internationally.

I started to hear about my friends or people I knew who were going to countries like the United States, England and Japan to do a Masters by way of a scholarship, or to work in South Korea, Poland or Switzerland. There seemed to be a widely accepted understanding that everywhere abroad had money growing on trees and pavements paved with coins, basically heaven under the sun. So, it was no wonder that we Mongolians itched to leave the country.

I didn't know what I really wanted at that time. I was happy and settled in my new job. I was trained as an English teacher and I was on the staff of the best English teaching school in Mongolia. The school was also the administration centre for IELTS test. I noticed my colleagues were eager to do the test and go on to study further abroad, doing their Masters or a PhD. Slowly, I was learning from my colleagues that doing well in the IELTS test meant a great deal in terms of opportunities to study abroad. All of the universities in English-speaking countries had their own language require-ments for their students. So, before I knew it, I was sitting a practice test with my colleagues.

The result was disappointing and frustrating. I had no fore-knowledge at all about the test. I hadn't anticipated that my result would be so bad that now I had put myself offi-cially at the bottom of the list compared to the other teach-ers in my school. I was the newest and youngest and now, I found, the worst of my colleagues in English language. It was embarrassing. So the management helpfully teamed me up with one of my native speaker colleagues called Bob. The idea was he would help me with speaking and understanding English and so on, and I would help improve his Mongolian. He would give me English magazines to read and we went to see films in English in a small family-sized cinema. He invited me to his flat and cooked onion soup once or twice. It was a bizarre experience to see someone making such a basic soup with minimal ingredients. Basically, we went eve-rywhere together. My English improved greatly and Bob's Mongolian was enriched, especially with my dialect and colloquial vocabulary. My colleagues would laugh at Bob's

Mongolian as his use of words was clearly directly derived from my vernacular.

Then, about four or five months later, it was time for Bob to go back to the UK. I was distraught as I'd really appreciated the help he'd given me with my confidence, as well as my English language skills; he had basically opened my eyes in so many ways. I was preparing properly for the IELTS test now. The school management proposed that I and one other teacher should sit IELTS with a view to reaching the score of 6.5. That would enable the school to send us to London on a professional development course, namely, a teacher-training course in a language school on Piccadilly in London.

I prepared for the test properly this time, working really hard. Now David was helping me with my English essays. I was rewriting passages so many times before I submitted the finished version to him. I was getting better as I was learning the exam techniques, following the tips on how to fill in answers and analysing what to look for when reading a passage. I would carry little pieces of paper with new words in my pockets and bags. Long lists of words were also placed all around my room and the bathroom. I was sleeping and dreaming in English, desperately trying to do well in my test. I needed to get my confidence back so that I could be good enough not only for the school, but also to be competent enough to apply for overseas university places for my Masters. I dreamt on...

THIRTEEN

Life-changing message

*Some people want it to happen,
some wish it would happen,
others make it happen.*

Michael Jordan

IT WAS JULY 2000 when Aeroflot flight SU 563 lifted off from Buyant-Ukhaa Airport in Ulaanbaatar, and I could feel my stomach fill with excitement and disbelief: 'Yes, I am on the plane to England! I will see the legendary Moscow first, the place I've seen only on TV and photos. I'm going abroad!' I'm sure if someone had had a camera in front of me they would have caught a huge grin on my face and wondered if I was unhinged. I wanted to nudge the person next to me and say, 'I'm going abroad. Can you believe it?!'

Who would have thought an email message that I wrote could have this power, not only to put me on a plane to London but also to change the rest of my life. I did not know much about British culture apart from the fact that London is the capital and there are four countries: England, Wales, Northern Ireland and Scotland. During the socialist time we were not allowed to talk about the capitalist countries. We had an image of capitalism as being bad and believed we were the lucky ones to be living in a socialist country. Things changed after Gorbachev and perestroika in the late 1980s, as we started to hear more about the West and many countries in the so-called developed world. It became possible to study more languages, including English, Chinese, Korean, Japanese, German and French instead of just compulsory Russian at school.

In my first-year English classes at university we memorised texts from our course book. I can still hear the bagpipes and see the Scottish man in his kilt on top of a mountain, beside a castle. I realised later, of course, that it was Edinburgh Castle. Now I was starting a life-changing journey, and all of the exercises in my English classes were coming to life. As a student and a teacher, I had practised so many times, rewinding and fast-forwarding the English tapes from our course book, trying to fill in the gaps in sentences. The subjects covered at the airport, at the train station, ordering food in a café and so on.

My English was put to the test when the stewardess asked what I would like to drink. She repeated the drink choices to everyone. I was thinking, 'Ok, I'll have water', preparing and practising to myself. 'Water, please.' 'Fizzy or still?' she continued and waited for my response. I wasn't prepared for that question, and had no idea what it meant. Sure, I had been out and about, going to places, ordering food and drinks, but only in Mongolia. I panicked and quickly said, 'Fizzy.' I was relieved that the conversation finished and she was happy with what I'd said. She gave me a bottle of water in a clear plastic cup, and I remembered that when we first became students one of our teachers said, 'Oh it's just wonderful to go abroad. You see, they give you cups and utensils that should be used once and thrown away. I felt like bringing them home for the kids to play with here.'

I tasted my water. It was disgusting. I had never tasted anything like that. It tasted salty. I couldn't take any more sips. I just pretended I had had enough, as if anybody cared. You see, I was trying to show people that I knew things. I was pretending I wasn't a country girl who knows only how to look after sheep and goats. I was one of those city girls who can tell who Madonna is and show off their pale skin.

After seven hours of flight we landed at Moscow's Sheremetyevo Airport. There, I was now in Moscow, taking my first step abroad outside Mongolia. I was so excited to see the Russian matryoshka dolls — I have several of them at my parents' home, bought for me by my uncles and aunts when I was little. I was buzzing with excitement and taking everything in. This massive airport was filled with the hustle and bustle of people of different nationalities and with different-coloured skin.

Once I had found out when my flight to London was and the gate number, I went around the duty-free shops. The shop assistants looked like dolls themselves with their perfect make-up and carefully selected clothes. Things looked very expensive and I decided not to buy anything to drink as it was $5 for a small bottle of water. I might not like it anyway if it was the same as the stuff I had tasted on the plane. After a few hours of waiting and gazing over lots of expensive things, I was in the queue to get on my next flight to London. Britain, here I come. I couldn't wait to see this world-famous London.

When the pilot announced we were about to land at Heathrow, I looked out of the window at the green carpet and the red roofs. Wow! It must be a big carpet, it's everywhere! No, it can't be carpet, it must be grass. How beautiful!

This journey wouldn't have happened at all if I hadn't bothered to write a short email message to London a few months earlier. My colleagues had all trained in England, Australia or America apart from me and another teacher. I prepared hard for the test and managed to get the score needed. To my disappointment the management now said they couldn't send me to London because they didn't have enough money. At first I didn't think of it much but when I explained what had happened to my other colleagues, who were older than me, they got angry and annoyed on my behalf, saying, 'That's not fair! You should do something about it.'

So I wrote an email message to the school that I was supposed to attend for my teacher training, explaining how much I wanted to go and expressing regret that it wasn't going to happen any more. I felt I couldn't lose anything by writing this message and sent it. A few days later, I received a reply from one of the directors of studies in the school. The message said: 'If you can make your way here, we are happy to give you a scholarship.' I was ecstatic. I announced this to everyone including my British friends, whom I had met through VSO (Voluntary Service Overseas). I could not believe it when one of them offered to pay for my flights and another paid for my room with a host family for a month in London. The course was for four weeks. So everything fell into place. I have to say I am grateful for what my friends did for me and I hope that one day I can do something similar for them or their children.

At Heathrow I was met by Bob and his friend Matt. It was like a dream. The streets were well lit and the reflection on the river and roads looked magical compared to the streets of my childhood in Sant, which were lit only by our torches. Here I was now, on an escalator, which I had only ever seen on TV and in films. Then I went on the Tube, the London underground. It was unreal. I used to stare at the postcards my dad brought from East Germany and dream about going abroad and travelling by 'metro', as I knew it.

Before long, it was time to start my course. My classmates were all from different countries, including Switzerland, Egypt, Taiwan, Brazil and Italy. The course was only for four weeks, but it was intensive. We had our own classes with our tutors in the mornings, then we taught English as a Foreign Language to students in the afternoon. We had two tutors. There were fantastic, and they made me realise that I can do many things. In fact, their praise and encouragement to think outside the box still play a big role in my confidence.

On the first Friday, there was a party in the school canteen, in the basement of the building. My classmates went downstairs to meet our tutors for a drink. As we entered the bar area, our tutor Robin was standing with his two other colleagues, chatting. 'We were just talking about you!' Robin turned to me and introduced me to the other colleague. Robin found it fascinating that I was from Mongolia and I was his first Mongolian student. One of the men, called Richard, was Scottish and in his late 20s. Richard ran the study centre in the school. He had lived and taught English in different countries including Ukraine and Poland. Richard and I started chatting and we exchanged business cards. Oh yes, I did have a bundle of business cards with me. One of my university friends had opened a small printing company just before I came to Britain and it was her present for me. I felt important, having my own business cards. Richard asked a lot of questions about Mongolia and we had fun dancing until midnight.

I was staying with a host family in Cholmeley Park in London, a retired couple with three grown-up children. They were warm and friendly and their youngest daughter, who was finishing school that year, was the only one still living at home with them. My host family thought I was very diplomatic and predicted that I would be the future Mongolian ambassador.

They talked to me about British culture and opened my eyes to all sorts of stuff. In one of our discussions over breakfast they told me about homosexuality. 'We have people in the parliament who are gay,' the wife informed me. The concept of homosexuality was hardly known in Mongolia, so I was listening to them very carefully with great interest. I couldn't name one person I knew who was gay.

A few days later, I made *buuz* Mongolian dumplings with beef for my host family for dinner. They were very pleased. Normally I only had breakfast with them as it was included in the price but not lunch or dinner. As I was serving the food their youngest daughter came home, beaming at being offered a place at Cambridge University to study music. I was so pleased for her and for them. They opened a bottle of wine and we all had a toast to congratulate the girl's achievement. It was good to have a proper meal that night and I told them that *buuz* was eaten in Mongolia to celebrate happy occasions.

Since arriving in London I'd had no idea where to go for dinner. It was like living on another planet. One evening I was so hungry on my way home that I went into a pub and asked if they had any soup, hoping that would fix my tiredness and hunger. The guy behind the bar nodded and told me to have a seat. There were a few men sitting at a table and they looked at me as if I was odd. I didn't care and waited for the soup. Soon, it arrived and I almost fell off my chair. It looked like leftover dirty water from after the dishes had been done. I stirred it with my spoon and tasted it slowly, unsure how it would be. There was no meat in it. How can soup be made without any meat? It tasted salt-free and bland. I had no idea what kind of soup it was, but I drank it anyway, taking the bowl in my hands and drinking it down. There was nothing in it that needed me to use a spoon anyway. The men at the other table stared at me as if I was doing something extraordinary. I'm glad I didn't lick the bowl as I would have done at home. I didn't buy anything else and left as soon as I had finished.

After that, I tried buying some food and drink myself. Once I bought a can of pâté and tried to open it and failed. I had no idea how to get it open. I looked at it for a while then turned the key, but obviously I did it the wrong way as I ended up breaking it. I was too embarrassed to ask my host family for help and chucked the whole thing in the bin unopened.

Another time, I bought a bottle of orange juice. I opened it and had a big gulp – it was truly strong and made me almost gag and my eyes twitch. So again, it went in the bin. Later on I realised it was a concentrated juice supposed to be diluted with water. I was not used to reading any labels on products or anything really. In Mongolia, most things were imported from abroad – from the former socialist countries like East Germany, Poland, Czechoslovakia, Russia and so on – and the labels were in different languages. So we were not used to reading instructions or recipes. The chances of knowing all of those languages were slim and we used guess-work based on our knowledge of Russian.

I was delighted when Richard asked me to go for dinner with him the day after we met. He knew where to go, and I agreed straightaway. We went to a Chinese restaurant in Soho the first night. The restaurant had chopsticks on the tables. I never got the hang of using chopsticks. We use spoons and forks at home. I looked at Richard thinking, 'What can I do?!' He didn't look comfortable either. We had a nice meal, though, and went out walking through the streets of London. Richard and I had dinner together for a few days and he took me round some of the tourist attractions. I had a great time getting my portrait done at Trafalgar Square, taking photos in Madame Tussauds with the Dalai Lama and with one of my favourite actors, Morgan Freeman. My days were getting numbered, though, and it would soon be time to return to Mongolia. Neither of us knew if we would see each other again. I felt comfortable around Richard and we were open and honest about our past and our thoughts on life.

Six weeks later, I was walking up and down the Arrivals lounge at Buyant-Ukhaa Airport in Ulaanbaatar, impatiently waiting for Richard's plane to land. It was November 2000 and Richard was coming to Mongolia for ten days to see me. I was glad that it had snowed the night before as it looked all clean and tidy in the streets. It was -28°C and much colder than Britain at that time. My aunt Gerlee Egch came to the airport with me to meet Richard and drove us to my bedsit in the city centre. Richard and I had been emailing each other since I had left Britain. He wanted to be with me and he was even willing to resign from his job in London to move to Mongolia. I did want to be with him, but it wasn't easy making any decisions at the time. My parents were still looking after Sara in Uliastai and my previous relationship hadn't worked out. I was scared to commit to anybody or any relationship, given that being with a foreign man was controversial then in Mongolia, and any woman holding hands or being seen with a foreign man was still frowned upon. So apart from my mum and my aunt Gerlee, my relatives knew nothing about Richard staying with me during his visit.

The days went quickly and it was soon time for Richard to go back. He wanted to give Sara a present. My mother was in Ulaanbaatar for a few days for a residential seminar around that time, thankfully staying outside the city, and Richard met her over lunch. He had bought a very pretty purple coat for Sara in the State Department Store. I was very touched by this gesture as Sara was the most important person in my life and I was not going to be with anyone who didn't accept her. My mum and Richard held a conversation through me, and Mum received the coat for Sara. I could tell my mum liked Richard, especially as he was so considerate towards her and softly spoken. He was ticking the boxes for her. He was educated and was also a teacher like her.

The night before Richard left we were in Khan Brau bar, which was owned by a German guy and his Mongolian wife. This bar was popular with my colleagues and I. Richard wanted to know about our future. I had still said nothing about being with him or living anywhere at that point. He must have felt it was like pulling teeth to get a word out of me about our relationship. To my horror, he started unbuttoning his shirt button and threatened me with a smile: 'I'm going to take off all my clothes and dance naked on the table if you don't tell me what you think.'

I was sure he was going to do it and ran off to the ladies toilet, imagining this embarrassing image and laughing at the same time. I watched him carefully from a distance as he calmly giggled to himself and took a sip from his beer. I returned with a cowardly look and sat down to explain.

'Look, I do want to be with you, but I already have a child. If things don't work out between us, it's all right for you. You can just go back. For me, it's different. I will have a reputation here for being with yet another man that things didn't work out with. A woman's reputation is vulnerable here.' I said it out loud. Richard had this effect on me. I found us talking honestly to each other, being straightforward. He appreciated my honesty and suggested I could come to London and improve my English. Even if things didn't work out, I would have gained from my experience of living in an English-speaking country.

Five weeks later, just before Christmas on 22nd December 2001, I landed in London to be with Richard, who had rented a house in Honor Oak Park in southeast London. The landlord, Ben, Richard's colleague who periodically travelled abroad for work, was a nice guy who lived in one of the rooms in the house. So my life in Britain started with English classes in Piccadilly in the mornings and job-hunting in the afternoons. It was frustrating, walking through the streets and going into every restaurant, pub, café and office, sometimes asking for work. I was totally dependent on Richard and, although I had everything I needed, I felt I didn't have my independence. Especially since being a teacher in Mongolia I was used to being respected and thought of as 'someone'. Here I was invisible.

After weeks and weeks of going from door to door and checking vacancies on Jobcentre boards I decided to go to a Mongolian restaurant in Covent Garden. I was exhausted physically and emotionally. I missed Sara dreadfully and there was no communication between me and my parents. I only used emails and MSN Messenger with some friends in Ulaanbaatar, and in Uliastai there was no internet connection at all. Mobile phones were new over there and my parents only had a landline. Richard tried to contact my parents through BT (British Telecom), but they said it would be £1.75 per minute and the operator said they had not communicated with Mongolia since the late 1990s.

I turned up at the Mongolian Barbeque restaurant hoping to eat something Mongolian and drink real Mongolian tea in an effort to relieve my homesickness. As it was during the afternoon, the restaurant was not open but the staff were already preparing for the evening. I went through the open door and asked if they had any jobs. They asked me to take a seat and wait for the manager. The restaurant was decorated with Mongolian décor and there were some Mongolian vodka bottles behind the bar. The waiting staff were not Mongolians, but they were friendly. Soon a cheerful guy in his 30s came out of a small office and shook my hand and introduced himself as Sam. He was South African and he took my details including my address. He exclaimed, 'You must be joking!' with a smile. He announced to the rest of the staff that his house was in the next street from where Richard and I were living. He informed me that he had just asked someone to leave that morning because of trust issues around money, so he was very happy to take me on and asked when I could start. I was over the moon and in a hurry to tell Richard my good news. Here was my first step to independence and settling into a new life and culture.

I was still new in the country and the whole experience was surreal. I had no idea how to cook or what to cook, even how to work a cooker or washing machine. Sure my parents had a washing machine, but we had to bring the water from the river, then empty the washing machine before rinsing the washing with clean water. The washing machines here, on the other hand, were easy to operate once you knew what buttons to press. Put the washing in, press the buttons and that's it. I was learning every day, from buying an underground ticket to not vacuuming Ben's room without his permission. It was a Mongolian thing to do. I cleaned the whole house including Ben's room and tidied his stuff while he was out. Richard almost had a heart attack when he realised what I had done. Luckily, Ben had been to a few countries including the Far East and he was all right with it. After that I learnt my lesson about privacy and personal space, which seemed a big thing in the Western world.

There were a few personal challenges too. I found it hard to accept that Richard had female friends. I had no problem with his male friends, but I used to get extremely jealous when Richard's female friends were around us. So much so that Richard had to warn his friends not to give him any hello and goodbye pecks on his cheeks or hugs. The friends must have thought I was a nightmare. My English was still poor and I couldn't understand their jokes or anything they referred to, such as their childhood TV programmes. So I felt I had nothing in common with them and I used to daydream about something else when their conversation started to be irrelevant to what I knew. The only TV programme I found easy to understand was *Blind Date*. Then, slowly, I started to tune into the language and the culture, day by day feeling less isolated and lonely. But my visa was about to run out and another decision needed to be made about our relationship. The difference in our personalities and cultural behaviour still constituted a massive gap.

Then, one day, Richard asked me how I felt about moving to Barcelona with him. He had been offered a job there doing more or less what he was doing in London. So we decided we would move to Barcelona and Richard resigned from his job in London.

After a bit of digging about for information, we realised I would have to go back to Mongolia to apply for my Spanish visa. So there we were, saying our goodbyes again, hoping we would see each other in Barcelona in a few weeks' time. I was glad too – I would get to see Sara.

FOURTEEN

The sea of happiness

If I get married, I want to be very married.

Audrey Hepburn

'NIGHT NIGHT. You have a big day tomorrow.' Margaret smiled at me. 'Your bed is in the study,' she added. She had asked Nan, the cleaning lady, to make up a bed for me there for the night as my uncle Baaba, who'd arrived from London that day for the wedding, was sleeping in the only other bedroom, Richard's old room. Baaba's family had moved to London because of his work the year before. We'd had a lovely dinner at a local Italian restaurant called the Battlefield Rest, on the south side of Glasgow. Then, Richard had gone back to our house to spend this, the night before our wedding, his last night as a single man, separate from me. It was a 6km walk. He wanted to enjoy this last period of freedom and to have time to think on his own. His friend Miguel was due to arrive from Switzerland later on and would be staying at ours with Richard.

I went upstairs and settled into the futon bed and my thoughts and memories took me into a different world. I could not bring myself to believe that I was actually getting married. I was getting married to Richard, my 'boyfriend', as they say in English. The concept of a 'boyfriend' had been a strange one a few years back. I remembered my parents talking to each other and Mum saying, 'Nowadays, these youngsters seem to live together before they get married properly.' Dad listened and added, 'In our time, we got married. That was it. No trial run.'

Well, Richard and I had had a couple of years of a 'trial run' and now we were finally getting married. I was 25 and Richard was 31. 'Just perfect,' Margaret, Richard's mum, would say about our age gap. I'd grown fond of Margaret when we'd stayed with her in the couple of months before we'd bought our own place. I recalled meeting her for the first time a couple of years previously. We'd flown in from London and had got in very late, after she had gone to bed. On the way from the airport, Richard's accent had started to change and he began saying words like '*aye*' instead of '*yes*'. The Scottish, the Glasgow accent it was. When we first entered his childhood house I felt this tingling feeling, which made me fall in love with the place. I looked around. It felt good to be there and I felt warmth and contentment. The wall clock looked like a star, or maybe a sunburst, and it ticked rhythmically as if to add a sense of calm and peacefulness. We went to bed in Richard's old room, where his belongings were stacked in the corner and the sign on the door said 'Richard's room' on a china nameplate with a picture of a toy plane on it. The light fitting had pictures of classic cars around it and there was a double bed carefully made up, especially for us.

The next morning, I came downstairs from the bedroom and met Margaret. This beautiful woman who had just turned sixty the day before greeted me with a huge smile. I was fascinated by her lovely blue eyes and her dangling purple earrings that moved from side to side every time she moved. She was sitting in her chair, which was facing a big TV in the corner. She switched off the TV and invited me to have a seat beside her. From then on, we saw each other pretty often, especially after we moved to Glasgow from Barcelona. Our Barcelona adventure hadn't lasted long as the weather was too hot for Richard and we found out that we could not get married there without having lived in the city for at least two years. So we decided to move nearer to his mother, who was on her own after she'd lost her husband shortly before. Also, she was not able to walk well because of the stroke she had had a few years back.

When we decided to come to Glasgow, Richard's friend Duncan and his girlfriend Anne kindly let us rent Duncan's flat in the city centre for a couple of months before we moved in with Margaret. I earned nothing and I was prohibited from accepting any public funds. So we mostly stayed in, sharing a tin of curry for dinner along with some boiled rice. Richard did a few hours' work every week for the company he'd worked for in Barcelona, via the internet, but that was our only income until he eventually managed to land a job in a local university. Hallelujah! We bought a little red car called a Nissan Micra. That was a great means of escape from the dark and *dreich* nights. The next big thing was buying our own home. We looked at a few places but it was hard to afford anything in the places we liked. Well, that Richard liked. I had no idea that different areas had different reputations and that all kinds of shenanigans such as drugs and violence were going on in certain parts of the city. Eventually, we found a house that we liked – albeit in an area that Richard wasn't so keen on. In May 2002, we moved into our first home. A television and a computer. Our suitcases. That was us. Two bedrooms, a box room, a living room, a small area for dining and a tiny kitchen that Richard and I couldn't both fit into at the same time. It didn't really matter, though, because I didn't know what to cook anyway, so we tended to eat ready meals such as pizzas that we could just put in the oven. Besides, I had grown up in a single-roomed round felt tent with a dung-fired cooking stove. So the lack of facilities in the kitchen did not bother me much.

We slept on the carpet for the first couple of nights. Then Duncan borrowed his father's car, which was bigger than our Micra, and helped us to collect a new bed from Ikea. Margaret gave us four plates, four forks, four spoons and four knives that we used while watching the television – which was propped on Richard's saxophone box. We may not have had much, but it was a really great moment in our life, starting out properly as a couple. That was a month ago now, and tomorrow we were finally getting married.

I remembered telling Richard just after we met that I would only get married to someone who would love my daughter, too. It was important for me to find someone trustworthy and genuine.

I liked Richard. He was very like me in many ways. He'd taught English as a foreign language in Ukraine and Poland, so he was aware of different cultures and he understood me when I felt homesick and had occasional cultural misunderstandings. We had a lot in common. Both of our mothers were teachers and our fathers did or had done responsible jobs. In other ways, too, our upbringing seemed very alike: it may have been quite strict but we were well looked after and encouraged to study and work hard. Saying all that, we did have our ups and downs and there were times when I felt that I didn't know if I could do this, living away from my daughter, trying to build a life with someone from such a different cultural background. On one occasion, I burst into tears in a pub because I was missing Sara, who was still in Mongolia with my parents, so much. But Richard was looking far ahead. He had already thought of bringing Sara over to be with us, and had considered which nursery to send her to – particularly as she was to start school the following year.

●

I woke up bright and early the next morning. The sun was shining as if in approval of our marriage and I felt good. When I went downstairs Margaret was up and in her chair, having already done her make-up. Her new turquoise suit brought out her eye colour and she looked *dead* smashing. It was her word and she had taught me to say '*dead*' to make any adjectives stronger. She would giggle and explain things for me happily. The girl who would be doing our hair had just arrived and she looked at me. 'So, what are you going to do with your hair?' she asked. 'Well, I'm going to wear a hat. So it would have to be down. Can you do breads? I mean braids? Or what do you call it? You know, when you do this.' I showed her what I meant, doing a little bit of my hair. 'They say *fish back* in Mongolia.' 'Oh, yes, yes. The fish-tail.' We were all glad that it was sorted. Kathy, Margaret's neighbour, had come in to help the bride get ready. 'What kind of hat are you wearing then?' the girl asked while finishing off my hair. I brought in my hat from the other room. It had been tailor-made for my wedding and had arrived from Mongolia just the day before. 'Oh, wow!' Kathy gasped and Margaret giggled with a knowing look. 'That's fantastic!' the girl added. 'So how do you wear it?' I put on my hat and the long dangling pearls and gemstones were so heavy that it was difficult to balance on my head. The ten peacock feathers on top made me look as if I was three metres tall. We managed to fasten it using the straps, which went under my hair – my hair itself was hidden behind a light pink train hanging from the back of the hat. I put on my grey silk *deel* with paisley patterns and slipped on my black shoes with tiny heels. I had asked my aunts in Ulaanbaatar to send me a hat for my wedding. I hadn't expected something quite so grand, with its jewels and peacock feathers and train. I was touched. I was picturing Byambaa Ajaa running round trying to organise a proper hat, calling everyone she knew and... Suddenly, I welled up, missing my mum and dad, and my relatives who couldn't be here with me. They would all have been made up and looking after me, laughing with me, making jokes and winding me up.

I stopped myself and turned around when Baaba entered the room. He exclaimed, '*Yamar goyo yum be naad malgai chin!*' meaning 'What a beautiful hat you have on!' I realised my Baaba was here, the oldest uncle of all my aunts and uncles, the most important one, to whom we all looked up. He was dressed up in his grey satin *deel* and wide leather belt with carved silver decorations. He also had his snuff bottle in its silk pouch and the sharp knife and the fire-making kit as worn in the olden days. It is a bit like the traditional Scottish sporran and the sgian-dubh. The difference was that Baaba's knife was attached to his belt in a decorated silver case with the handle visible whereas the Scottish way is to wear the sgian-dubh tucked into the top of the kilt hose (long Scottish socks), with only the upper part of the handle visible.

The doorbell rang. 'Oh, the car's here,' Kathy announced as she opened the door. 'I'm going to tell the girls and they can come out and see the beautiful bride.' She giggled and left. Our wedding was at 10 o'clock at the Park Circus Registry Office in the west end. While holding onto my wedding hat I followed Jess, Margaret's close friend. I saw this beautiful, shiny burgundy-coloured Daimler outside the gate and a smartly dressed chauffeur opened the door with his white-gloved hand and invited me in. After a bit of trouble trying to fit myself into the car with my tall peacock feather hat, I gave up and took it off and sat it on my lap. Margaret, Baaba and Jess settled in beside me and Kathy and her little girls waved to us as we drove off around the corner.

For a moment, my memories flooded in. In Sant, I've been to many weddings and it is always a huge event because of the large families and close-knit community, with everybody knowing each other. Wedding days are chosen according to the lunar calendar and, consequently, many weddings take place on the same day. Every village has its own traditions and rituals. In Sant, the groom's family prepare almost everything including the new *ger*, the bride's dress and shoes for the wedding day. I loved the smell of the new *ger* with its fresh wooden frame and the new felt covers. The atmosphere was always magical, with everyone in a happy mood and children running around with sweets in their hands.

'It's the only dry and sunny day this week,' Margaret smiled. 'Oh I know, it poured for the last few days. It has cleared up for Uuganaa and Richard's wedding,' Jess nodded. 'Yes, for a special couple, it's a special day,' Baaba added. I was happy to see the sun and took in the atmosphere of the city as we reached the registry office.

I had been told that Richard and I were not supposed to see each other before the ceremony. So Baaba and I waited in a room until a guy invited us to enter a grandly decorated hall. I slowly walked down the aisle with Baaba as the music came on. Richard was wearing his kilt and full Scottish gear, standing beside Alan, the best man. Alan was dressed in the same traditional clothes but his plaid kilt pattern was different. It was only later that I learnt that brides have bridesmaids and flower girls here. I didn't know any of that and, besides, I didn't yet know many people here. In Mongolia, the equivalent of bridesmaids are *bergen*. They are the people who look after the bride during their wedding day and are chosen and matched according to the appropriate horoscope year.

With Baaba beside me, I felt happy and content. The registrar stood behind a grand mahogany desk and asked Richard and I to repeat the words after her. Looking into each other's eyes, holding each other's hands, we put our rings on one another's fingers – they were not extravagant but we had bought them for one another and they were a simple symbol of our marriage. We had put together a CD of songs we would like to be played on our wedding day, and in the background the song 'Chiquitita' by ABBA played in Spanish – as if it was not culturally diverse enough already to have a wedding in a traditional Mongolian hat and *deel* and a Scottish plaid kilt!

As soon as we had finished the photo shoot, my parents called from Uliastai. Baaba and I spoke to them and Richard had his turn to say '*Bayarlalaa*', meaning 'Thank you' for their good wishes. My dad hadn't even met Richard at that point. He asked Baaba about us, how we were living, and about Richard's background and personality. We then headed to the Sherbrook Castle Hotel in the south side of Glasgow for our wedding lunch. There were about fifteen people altogether, including Richard's friends and his uncle Billy, his cousin Douglas and my friends Ishbel and Ian, whom I had originally met in Mongolia.

Baaba made a speech and offered us milk in twin silver bowls, holding them draped in blue Buddhist silk scarves. The ritual is to take a sip from the milk and pass it on in a clock-wise direction until everyone has had a sip. Then Alan made his speech, which included references to some of Richard's most embarrassing moments. It also pointed out how careful he was, making Alan check if the house was locked that morning seventeen or eighteen times, then checking the rings twenty times. He invited everyone to raise a toast to us: 'To Richard and Uuganaa.' The next speaker was Margaret, almost in tears, 'I couldn't have asked for a nicer daughter-in-law, not only beautiful but pleasant-natured with it. Thank you Richard!' The room filled with 'Awws' and handclaps. She would later tell me that she had already told her friends 'I want that girl to be my future daughter-in-law' the day after we met: and there I was, becoming just that. She also wanted me to have a Scottish accent. That was still to come.

After our lunch we headed for the airport to fly to London for some more celebrations. Alan drove us in his car and still in our wedding gear we got on the plane.

We arrived in London with Miguel, Alan and Baaba. My aunt Dulma Egch and cousin Enkhe met us with a beautiful bouquet of flowers and champagne at their home in Kensington. Then we all went to the language school where Richard and I had first met. The school was kindly allowing us to hold a party. After all, as Baaba pointed out in a friendly way in his speech later on, 'It was the school's fault.' Richard's old colleagues and my tutors threw confetti from the balcony as we arrived in Piccadilly. I loved the fact that they had had fun preparing for our arrival by making confetti from their hole punches. They had laid on a beautiful wedding reception buffet for us. I was told later that the traffic in Piccadilly slowed down as people wanted to see us in the street.

My university teacher David's friend Freddie and his wife Claire were among the many guests. Also, Bataahai, an old schoolfriend from Sant, who had turned up smartly dressed. Baaba and Alan made their speeches and Bataahai sang 'Хөөрхөн Халиун', a Mongolian folk song.

ХӨӨРХӨН ХАЛИУН ДОШГИН ШҮҮ

ХӨЛД НЬ СУУЖ Л БАРИАРАЙ

ХҮНИЙ ГАЗАР ХЭЦҮҮ ШҮҮ

ХҮЛЭЭН БАЙЖ Л ДАСААРАЙ

ХАЧИН ХАЛИУН ДОШГИН ШҮҮ

ХАЗААРЫГ НЬ ТАТАЖ БАЙЖ МОРДООРОЙ

ХАРИЙН ГАЗАР ХЭЦҮҮ ШҮҮ

ХАЙРЛАН БАЙЖ Л ДАСААРА

The song is about someone living far away in a foreign land, and how important it is to be patient and loving in order to get used to the place and make it one's own. It was a fitting song and particularly touching. Bataahai was in the class below me in Sant and now here we were in London, on the other side of the world. Once previously, when I had been living in London, I had gone to see him in tears as I was missing Sara so much. I had called him on his mobile, sobbing, and he had said, 'Come to our flat and I will cook lamb noodle soup for us.' That was a hard time, trying to get used to the culture in London with so little experience of living or travelling abroad.

Our wedding day ended with us going to a hotel in Mayfair. It was a long day, but a great one. I'm Mrs Ramsay now, like Margaret. She is my mother-in-law. I wanted to call her Mum like they do in Mongolia, but Richard thought it was weird. Maybe not.

<hr>

After spending about four 'honeymoon' days in Bangor in Wales we returned to normality in Glasgow. The next thing on the list was to bring Sara over. At the time, I was working in a hotel in the west end of the city as a receptionist, doing shifts. Richard would drive me to work at about 6am for the morning shifts then pick me up at about 11pm from the evening ones. It would make sense if I could drive myself. My mother-in-law kindly paid for a few driving lessons for me to get started. I had never, ever tried to drive before, never mind in a foreign city, one of the busiest in Scotland at that, with many steep hills. My driving instructor had to change one of the tyres during my first lesson as I hit the kerb and the rim came off, leaving him with a dirty job facing some dog poo. After a few driving lessons, I had learnt that the word for dog shit in Glasgow is '*jobby*' and I could now manoeuvre a car along the road without damaging the rim of the tyres. Even better, when I sat my theory test, not only did I pass, but I got one hundred per cent. It was a different story though when it came to the practical test. I tried to go straight through a red light and so failed my first test. The second time was better. 'I PASSED!' I screamed on the phone to Richard and Margaret and then called my parents. With my driving licence came the pleasure of freedom. I didn't have to depend on Richard's good nature any more.

Then it was time to think about bringing Sara from Mongolia. I had prepared my parents for the wrench as much as I could. I knew they would miss her, but they also couldn't say no to me. They prepared Sara, too. At that stage she was just four and she looked forward to seeing her *aav,* meaning 'Dad'. She was excited to see her house that had stairs inside and non-stop electricity and her own new separate room – all concepts that she had not experienced before. When my parents heard that Sara would be sleeping all on her own in a room – she had slept in the same bed as my mother until now – they were concerned, but they felt they couldn't object. Richard and I sent a video tape from our wedding that also had a tour of our house, so they could see the room that Sara was to have, to try to reassure them. I also showed them what pizza was, explaining that it is similar to Mongolian *gambir* and had a few strips of vegetables and ham on it.

In February 2003, I flew to Uliastai via London, Moscow and Ulaanbaatar with the Russian airline Aeroflot then the Mongolian airline MIAT. I spent about ten days with my parents before returning to Glasgow with my daughter. As we left Uliastai, I could feel my parents' emotion and I knew they were holding themselves together. They gave me money to buy new clothes for Sara from Ulaanbaatar on the way and gave her a pair of little golden earrings for the time when she got her ears pierced. As a traditional way of wishing us a good journey, Mum brought some milk in a metal container and sprinkled some into the air after us with a carved wooden ladle attached to a blue Buddhist scarf. I could see them still doing it until we couldn't see them any more. My dear parents' unconditional and endless love sets us among the luckiest people in the world.

Sara was well behaved on the flights, sleeping on my lap and eating happily. She was enjoying this experience enormously. She was with her mummy now and she was going to her *aav*, the man with a big Western nose and long hair (Richard's hair reached his shoulders). After arriving at Heathrow, we stayed at Baaba's in London for a night and got on the train to Glasgow the next day. After a very long last leg of the journey that took eight hours instead of about five, we finally got to Glasgow at about 9pm on 23rd February 2003. Richard carried Sara, who had fallen asleep on the train, to the car and she woke up on the way home. As soon as we got there, Richard took her to show her her little room. He had decorated it with colourful balloons and had put a toy dog from Margaret on the bed. I was touched by this lovely gesture and was proud of my husband. Richard also pointed at the *Very Hungry Caterpillar* book on our TV and said, 'That's yours, too.' '*Aav, yu gej baina?*' Sara turned to me. I explained the book was hers. '*Za,*' she smiled. Since then, Richard and Sara have taught each other and learnt from one another, without needing me to interpret for them. Sara's English got better day by day thanks to cartoons like *Dora the Explorer*, *Scooby Doo* and *Angelina Ballerina*, and to the nursery at Richard's work.

Six months later, my little girl was starting school. Posing in her new white shirt, grey pinafore and black shiny shoes with flowers on them, she suddenly looked such a big girl. Richard dropped us off at the school gate and Sara joined the queue with her new classmates. I felt so proud and took a few photos of her.

I desperately needed a different job now. With Sara being here, I couldn't do shifts any more. I applied for jobs every day but I was only receiving rejection letters and I started to lose hope and confidence. I remembered feeling important and valued as a teacher. Knowing and speaking the language wasn't enough, though. I needed to learn the culture, get used to the accent, make myself understood without any mistakes and, most importantly, I desperately needed to discover the trick of actually getting the job that you applied for. It was no problem learning how to fill in the application forms – sticking to the same format, using the words from the job adverts and matching them with your skills and qualities – and I was getting a few job interviews. But now I had to learn how to perform in the interview. 'Why do you want this job?' 'I really need it': the bad answer. 'I love working with people from different backgrounds...': better answer. I read up about everything from having nice clean teeth to preparing a presentation. So I went for every job interview

I could and learnt from each of them. Richard was very supportive and he blamed himself for bringing me here when, in Mongolia, I'd had a proper job, my family and friends, in fact, everything else except him. Then I had a phone call from an ex-colleague from the hotel, Katya, a Brazilian lady who had recently changed jobs and was now working with ethnic-minority groups. She asked if I wanted to do a computing course at a local college almost in our street. It was a godsend. I enjoyed the course and applied for a job at the college as a student adviser and was offered an interview. The usual rejection letter came, so I went to see the manager of the student advice centre, Mary. It seemed that the reason I wasn't selected was that I had no experience in this country. 'Well, can I work for you for no pay for a month, please? That would be an experience.' I don't think Mary expected that. 'Yes, let me speak to some people.'

A week later, I was in the student advice centre preparing their student induction presentation for the new academic year. The principal, who incidentally became the Boss of the Year in the UK that year, allowed me to work there without pay, which gave me the chance to show what I could do. While I was working there an administration job came up and I got it. My thirty-third interview! Richard had been counting them. I was so relieved. It was an easy job and I found myself doing most of the work within a couple of days, so I started a course in counselling skills within the college.

After a couple of years working at the college, Richard and I decided it was time to try for a baby. In October 2004 we moved house to a seaside town where our kids could run around and play in the fresh air at the sandy beach. I spent the day with my mother-in-law shopping for some wool so that she could knit a little cardigan for the baby, who was expected the following April. She asked, 'Which colour do you prefer?' I picked some light blue wool and she bought that. I didn't realise then that boys and girls wear different colours here and I had inadvertently chosen a colour for a baby boy.

Richard didn't let me do anything as soon as I was pregnant. I was told off when I lifted a dining chair as it was too heavy for me and he would run around and do that kind of thing for me. I enjoyed the attention and my mother-in-law giggled and supported me in every way. Sara was excited at the prospect of seeing her new sibling.

Richard and his mum couldn't wait to find out if we were having a boy or a girl and we waited impatiently for the ultrasound scan day. In Glasgow, the hospitals didn't tell parents the sex of the baby for ethical reasons as some families had a preference, whereas, where we lived now, they were happy to tell us. The day came and the radiographer said, 'Oh, it's a wee lad.' We were over the moon. We were just happy. I don't think we had any real preferences for a boy or a girl, but knowing was good. Of course, the wool I had chosen was a boy colour and the new granny-to-be was soon knitting away at a little cardigan.

So there I was, settled in a new house, waiting for a new baby, and my sister Zaya was on her way to visit for the first time.

●

July 2009. I strolled along the street to the park at the beach watching Simon on his scooter. It was a lovely sunny morning and Simon was already four. He was an early riser just like I was. It was the weekend and Richard and Sara were not up yet. My mother-in-law had moved down to be near us and now lived only 10 minutes' walk down the road.

Simon was named after my father-in-law. He also had a Mongolian name, Dalaibayar. I didn't understand why people give their parents' names to their kids here. In Mongolia, it's a bad sign. They say it might be too heavy for the child to carry, meaning the child might become ill or something bad might happen to them. For Simon's Mongolian name, we had consulted my parents. A few days after my birth I had been named Uuganbayar, meaning 'first happiness', by my father. We decided Simon could take some of my name – *bayar* (which means 'happiness') – and, as we were beside the sea, *dalai*, 'sea'; Dalaibayar means 'sea of happiness'. The sea would be a spiritual representation, respect for the sea, which would be gentle and look after us.

By now, I had educated myself to another level, doing a postgraduate degree and becoming a careers adviser. As such, I had changed jobs a few times, working in different local schools and colleges. I was settled in Scotland, especially now in this seaside town, and everything was just perfect.

That day, I noticed the ice-cream kiosk lady opening her shop and she gave me a wave. Simon and I are regular customers, buying ice-cream and sitting at the ballast stone wall to watch life go by. Sara is mostly a fan of candy floss, or sometimes a 99 ice-cream, the one with a Flake chocolate bar in it. She loves the raspberry sauce. So does Simon. He especially enjoys it when his face is smothered in the brightly coloured sauce, and people walk by giggling at him and making comments like, 'Is that nice?'

My parents were both here for a visit and now they were happy that they'd seen us in a world very different from theirs. We were content in our little family. Simon came and looked at my belly. 'Mummy, when is the baby coming out?' 'November, Simon. You'll have a baby brother. Isn't that lovely?' 'Yes, Mummy,' he nodded.

FIFTEEN

Where is God?

If God lived on earth, people would break his windows.

Jewish Proverb

IT WAS 25TH JANUARY 2010: for most Scots, the anniversary of Robert Burns's birth. In our family it's my mother-in-law's birthday. We would normally take her out for lunch, but this year her health had deteriorated rapidly. She was now in a nursing home, unable to fend for herself.

You would have thought that there was enough going on, having a baby with Down's syndrome and a heart defect. But, on top of that, Sara had burnt her leg really badly a couple of weeks previously. Sara's burn was deeper than we expected and she'd been admitted to a bigger hospital an hour's drive from our town a few days ago.

So now, on Rabbie Burns Day, here I was leaving home in the morning with Billy to go and visit Sara before her skin-graft operation. Simon stayed with Richard, who was working from home that day. After driving for an hour we finally got to the hospital. I went around the car park and couldn't find anywhere to park the car. It was almost 11am. I was late for Sara. The nurses had told me to be there about 11am as Sara would be going into theatre at 11.15am. I had to park the car on a yellow line and run as fast as I could, pushing Billy in his pram in the pouring rain. Billy had his feeding tube in his nose and he had been discharged from a local hospital only two days earlier. So, the previous week, we'd had had two children in two different hospitals.

We flew upstairs and saw Sara in her room with a sign on the door saying 'No food or drink' in preparation for the operation. She looked pale and tired. Billy woke up and started looking around, checking out the high ceiling and large windows. Now that Billy was awake, Sara had a cuddle. She adored her brothers. She used to rush home from school, in a hurry to see Billy. She had done the same with Simon a few years earlier. She was so happy to hold her baby brother, her eyes all gooey. Billy enjoyed her attention – his lips would be moving and he would look as though he wanted to say something. These were precious moments. After some cuddles, feeding Billy through the tube, which was placed through his nose, and changing his nappy, it was time for Sara to be taken to the operating theatre.

While Sara was in theatre, we had to fill in a form with a member of the Family Support Team. 'I apologise, we have to ask some questions: do you have a social worker?' Thinking of Billy, I answered, 'Not yet.' I think the woman thought I was being sarcastic and she started apologising again. I said, 'No, I mean it. We probably will have a social worker some time soon. Having two children being ill and we already needed support.' I couldn't believe how life could change. I had worked with social workers in relation to my students, but I had never imagined that I would need one myself. You just never know what's around the corner.

While we were there, I noticed that Billy was coughing from time to time and he looked as though he was in pain. So I decided to take him down to Accident and Emergency as soon as Sara had come out of theatre. My sister-in-law came to visit Sara. It was nice of her. I had had to text a few people when Sara was admitted to hospital. I was worried that she would have nobody visiting her or calling her on the phone. It's hard at times like this. If I was in Mongolia, my relatives would have visited her in turns and she would have been spoilt rotten with presents and sweets. My sister-in-law was praising Sara, telling her what a brave girl she was. Sara started to fill up, and tears started to roll down her cheeks. I couldn't do anything, though, as, right in the middle of everything, I was feeding Billy through his tube. I can be very bad at times like this. I was stressed out and annoyed that my sister-in-law's praise had made Sara feel emotional, and now she was crying. I told Sara off, saying, 'Don't cry, you'll get a headache. You haven't drunk much today.' I continued, 'It'll be fine. It's just skin, it's on the outside. It'll heal quickly.' I sounded mean and harsh. I didn't like it myself, but I just had to do it. We couldn't go on crying and making everything into a drama. It was very hard for me to be so unsympathetic to Sara, but inside I knew Billy was in a serious situation, as he was now looking blue.

After giving Sara a drink and some toast I told her that I was going to take Billy downstairs. My sister-in-law had left earlier on. I went to the Accident and Emergency desk and a friendly guy in his mid-50s looked at Billy and took the details. 'Have a seat and someone will be with you shortly.' He directed me with his eyes towards the seating area. It was busy there with many children and parents; there was a big television screen on the wall and some toys on the floor. I spotted a free seat but just as I was about to sit down, I heard, 'William R...!' That was quick! I thought we would have to wait for a while considering the number of other people also waiting. Instead, the nurses and doctors started to run around Billy, connecting him up to various pieces of equipment. 'Is he normally this blue? Blue babies worry us,' they were conferring with each other. Then someone new would come, introduce himself and join the team. Billy was put on oxygen. After an hour or so we were told that they wanted to keep him in overnight for observation. So we moved to a temporary room with other children who were also waiting for beds. I was worried about Sara. I hadn't thought it would be so long and so serious. I asked one of the nurses if I could go and see my daughter upstairs, leaving Billy there in his cot, still on oxygen.

I checked my mobile and there were 23 missed calls from Sara and a few text messages. 'Mum, where are you? I need the toilet, I can't walk.' 'Mum, where are you??????? I need you!!!!!' I ran through the corridors and up the stairs. She was upset because I hadn't got back to her sooner. She felt I had abandoned her. She was right. I'd disappeared as soon as she came out of theatre, half-conscious and with no feeling below her waist. I felt terrible and guilty.

'Where is Billy?' she asked, noticing that I had returned on my own. 'He is downstairs in a different ward. They are keeping him there for the night. So I'll be here too. I'll come and go between you two.' 'Why? Why are they keeping Billy here?' 'He has a cough,' I said, trying to make light of it. I didn't want to worry her. She is a sensible and considerate big sister. It broke my heart when, just the day before, she had said to me, 'Mum, go home. I'm not the only one who needs you.' She was right again: Billy was just out of hospital and Simon had had a high temperature the night before. My poor little girl, only 11 and already thinking selflessly like this. I spent a little while with Sara, made her a glass of diluted orange juice and then ran back to Billy.

Billy was content, sucking on his dummy, which was supported by his little toy monkey that Richard had bought him – Billy's first toy. I sat beside him stroking his hand, talking to him in Mongolian. At about 9pm we were taken up to the ward where Billy was staying that night. The room was on the ninth floor and had a beautiful view but no toilet. As Billy was being admitted to hospital, I had to fill in some more forms. I felt annoyed and resentful of the bureaucracy when I had so much on my mind and wanted to focus all my attention on my baby, instead of answering their questions, especially as some of them didn't seem at all relevant to Billy or his health.

After I had completed the paperwork and settled Billy in, I went downstairs to the fourth floor to see Sara again and give her a goodnight kiss. She was much better but still looked very tired. I stayed with her for a while and then went outside to park the car somewhere safe. As I approached the car I noticed something yellow under the windscreen wiper. Oh no! I had a parking ticket. I couldn't believe it. But there was nothing I could do other than move the car, now that there were free spaces, and go back to Billy.

As I entered the ward, the same nurse commented that Billy was a 'wriggly baby' and that the alarm kept coming on. I saw that he was extremely restless, fidgeting and covered with sweat. Something was wrong. My instinct as a mother drove me to try to do something about it. I fed Billy through his tube and he was sick immediately. God, help me. I pressed the call button. One of the nurses came in and I blurted, 'There is something wrong. He does sweat, but not like this.' Once we had cleaned him up and changed his bedding Billy fell asleep. The nurse came back in, this time querying Billy's diuretics doses. I had actually told her earlier, but she was checking it with me again. She wanted to speak to Richard at home to check the strength of the medicine. We had left it all at home. We hadn't expected to be admitted to hospital today, as we were intending only to visit Sara. I phoned Richard and the nurse spoke to him.

Finally, I dozed off, but I was then woken up by the same nurse and the consultant in charge that night. It was about 1am. They were apologetic in their manner, saying, 'We are really sorry, but it now appears that his dosage of diuretic has been incorrect.' In my fragile state, I had very mixed feelings, but I tried to concentrate on a positive outcome. Please God, help us.

The next morning, everything seemed to be going according to plan. Sara was happier and Billy was still on his fluids to correct the overdose and oxygen. The day shift had started, and the nightmare seemed to be fading with the daylight. The doctor came in for the ward round and said that they would check Billy again once his fluids were finished. I asked the nurses if I could go home to get a change of clothes. I had had to borrow a gown from the hospital as I didn't have any other clothes apart from what I was wearing when I'd left home the day before. After checking with the doctor I was allowed to go home.

As I got home, after driving for an hour, I felt shattered. I hadn't had time to feel just how tired I was, but still I couldn't afford the time to lie down or relax with a cup of tea. I threw the parking ticket on the dining table and said to Richard, 'Please don't be annoyed with me – I have a ticket.' He just went online and paid the fine, sorted it out. He knew exactly how I was feeling. He was equally frustrated. At home with Simon he had been worried sick about the three of us in hospital, while still trying to work. I ran upstairs and started putting some clothes in a bag. The phone rang. 'Hello. Is that Mrs R...?' 'Yes' 'Just to let you know that William is being transferred to the High Dependency unit. No rush. Go to High Dependency when you come. He will be there.'

Tuesday, 23rd February. Billy had been in the Intensive Care unit for four weeks, teetering on the edge of life and death. The phone call I'd received a month ago had directed me to go to the High Dependency unit; however, by the time we'd turned up he was in the Intensive Care unit. My ginger-haired tiny baby boy was completely surrounded with high-tech equipment and machines, lying in a metal cot. On one side of his nose he was connected to a ventilator, and he had two feeding tubes on the other. They had been using a catheter from time to time to help him urinate and he had another draining tube in his tummy. Billy's heart was struggling and he was retaining more and more body fluid. He looked distended, as if he had been pumped up. His skin looked so thin, almost like a balloon about to burst. His arms and legs were covered with needle marks and plasters holding IV lines. On the inside, I felt like holding onto the cot and breaking down in tears. From the outside, I just about managed to look strong.

We were not allowed to stay with Billy overnight. Many parents seemed to stay during the day and then go home in the evenings. Richard was still trying to work every day and I was at home with Simon. Sara started going back to school. Her leg was getting better but we still had several appointments to check that the skin graft and the donor site were both healing properly. Also, she had to wear a special garment for a year.

As soon as Simon's nursery had started in the afternoon I would rush to hospital, driving as fast as the speed limit allowed, with the radio up full blast. One day I heard Snow Patrol's 'Run' and listened at top volume. As the singer sang that he was *right beside you, dear* – even if 'dear' couldn't hear his voice, the words perfectly fitted my mood.

Every day I visited Billy in Intensive Care, but only for an hour or so as I had to be back for Simon and the driving took an hour each way. I would try to find out as much as I could about what was happening to Billy and write down the name of every medicine he was taking. As soon as I got home I would Google them and find out as much as I could. Richard was doing the same. I don't know how he managed to carry on working during this period. I guess it was a distraction and something else to focus on. We did not know how long Billy would be in hospital and our sense of normality had completely changed. Richard had to work to take care of us, his family, especially now with a disabled child.

It was 23rd February, about 3pm. Richard and I were taken into a room with a window by the consultant, cardiologist, neurologist, cardiac nurse and the Intensive Care nurse who was looking after Billy that day. They had tried to choose a bright room to talk to us. I had my notepad and a pen, preparing to write down what they were about to say. This meeting had been postponed for days. We had spoken to each of these specialists on different occasions, but had been told to wait till this meeting, when they were all together.

I felt very angry and annoyed inside when we had finally found out, almost by accident, that Billy had brain damage, cerebral palsy, on top of everything else. Nobody had told us about it until one of the doctors dropped it in, in the middle of a conversation. 'Obviously because of his brain situation…' he carried on. I was bemused. 'Clearly, you have known about this for a couple of days at least.' 'Nobody has told us anything about it.' The doctor found himself in an awkward situation and said simply, 'Yes.' Later, we were actually grateful for how this doctor behaved throughout, but at the time I was stressed out and like a wolf protecting my cubs.

We were now apprehensive about this big meeting, though I still hoped they would tell us that we would have our three children playing at the beach that summer. The cardiologist started. 'William's future looks bleak. We have options. The decision is yours.' He spoke very carefully and slowly, observing us. We sat round in a circle. Richard sat on my left. The cardiologist continued, telling us how Billy's heart was not functioning well, especially on the right side. He also pointed out that Billy's lungs were totally dependent on the ventilator and on top of that he had a chest infection. Billy's stomach had a virus and was not processing his feeds... the list went on. 'We thought these four weeks would show us if William could possibly make a turn around and get better. Unfortunately, things have gone from bad to worse.' My notes stopped. I started doodling madly, biting my lip, desperately trying not to cry, swallowing my tears, trying to be brave, falling apart inside, but just about holding myself together. Richard's tears started rolling down his cheeks. After half an hour of questions and answers they left us alone in the room. We hugged each other and cried together for a while. The big window in the room seemed to be there only to show that the world was still outside, churning its guts with strong wind and driving snow.

We had to decide whether or not Billy would go through with the heart operation. According to the doctors, our Billy was going to die, and the operation couldn't realistically make much difference. Billy would probably not survive it and, even if he did, he would end up in a vegetative state.

Richard and I both knew the decision we had to make. We did not need to discuss it. We both knew and agreed that we would say goodbye to Billy in our arms rather than on an operating table. The doctors said, 'We will keep William as comfortable as we can.'

We left the hospital in the early evening and went to Scotts, a restaurant at the harbour near our house. We could not go home in our present state to see Sara and Simon. We needed some time to take in the news and pull ourselves together. I phoned my parents from my mobile and broke the news. Soon my uncles and aunts started ringing my mobile one after another. I could not speak to most of them and decided not to answer their calls. I realised I could not tell them again and again what was going on and hear them saying, 'Be strong.' I spoke to them in Mongolian, which made me feel the entire situation even deeper. I felt even more emotional in my mother tongue, and I just could not handle it. It was too much. My throat felt constricted, like I might choke.

SIXTEEN

Goodbye Billy

The trick is to keep breathing.

Janice Galloway

AFTER HAVING SOME TIME to take in the news in the restaurant, finally we went home. Since the situation was so extreme, the hospital had suggested that either or both of us could stay with Billy. So I went back to the hospital with my friend Jackie. We have only one car, and I thought Richard and the kids might need it. So Jackie gave me a lift. It's good to have Jackie. She had made it easy for me to settle into life in Scotland. She has always been there for me and all of us.

When we arrived at the hospital, Billy looked even more blue and fragile. He was kept asleep all of the time. I couldn't cope with him being upset. Once they were weaning him off his morphine, he was more awake. But when he cried, he made no sound. All I could see was that his face looked as though he was crying and his lips were curled as if he was hurt that I was not holding him. I could not hold him, even though I wanted to kiss him, cuddle him and hold him tight against me. I had not been able to hold him for a month as he was being kept alive only by the ventilator. I could not even get a good kiss on his cheeks. The cot was too high for me and I would stretch across, battling my way through the various cannulas and wires. I couldn't handle seeing Billy upset. I begged the nurse to give him more morphine; I didn't want Billy to be in pain. I would talk to him in Mongolian and English. I sang Mongolian lullabies to him while stroking his head.

Jackie looked at Billy and then she got upset, hugging me, saying, 'You are so strong, I'm sorry.' After a while, Jackie left. I sat there beside Billy, watching over my beautiful boy, spending our last moments together. I had been defending him and his condition since he was born. I was ready to leave everything, and to live with him somewhere far away from other people's judgemental attitude and selfish comments.

I sat there until 1am and felt a really bad headache coming on. I could not see properly. My eyes stung from fatigue, and from the salt of constant tears. I said, 'I'll have a nap for an hour,' to the young nurse who was looking after Billy that night. The Intensive Care unit had a family room and they put a bed in there for me that night. I could not sleep, though. I just tossed and turned.

I was startled by footsteps running towards the door and then heard a panicked hammering knock on the door over the corridor from me. 'Please come to the ICU now,' a woman's voice called to the consultant in a panic. Then the door opened and closed, with another set of running footsteps fading away in a hurry. I instinctively thought, 'It's Billy.' I jumped out of bed, blaming myself for not being there, and ran to the area where Billy was.

A few doctors and consultants were around Billy. Then they saw me and asked me to wait. My heart started to race.

'Is he all right?' 'Please, please, please be all right.' After a few minutes I was allowed to go and see Billy. He looked stable. But I could tell he hadn't been just before. The nurses and doctors looked relieved. I was told they had brought him back. I was so, so, so grateful. One of the nurses had brought Billy back. We had almost lost him. I thanked God.

The consultant in charge spoke to me. They were not confident that they could bring Billy back if the same thing happened again. They'd had to use adrenaline, their last resort. I called Richard. 'Hi. You need to come, we almost lost Billy. I'll call Jackie and she can be with the kids. I'll phone a taxi for you.' Then I called Jackie. She went straight to our home. What would we have done without Jackie?

Richard came to the hospital about 3.30am by taxi. The consultant spoke to us again and suggested that we should bring Billy's baptism forward. We had planned to have it at 10am that morning. Richard's friend Alan had arranged it with his church minister. The consultant was worried that Billy would not make it to 10 o'clock. The hospital chaplain was available and she came at 5am after a phone call. There we were, in the middle of the Intensive Care unit, the curtains around us, and Billy was baptised. I didn't really have much knowledge or experience of baptism. Mongolia's major religion is Buddhism, although I'm not the most religious person in my family. The chaplain asked if I needed any other religious support. I asked if it was possible to find a Buddhist monk.

We were moved to a separate room on our own to say our goodbyes to Billy in the Intensive Care unit. It was almost like a military operation to move him because of all the machines and equipment, all connected to one another. It took five nurses to do it: two pushing the cot, another pushing the stand with the screens and monitors, someone else carrying the battery supplying the power for all the

equipment, including the ventilator, and the last one dragging along the medicine stand. Richard and I followed with
Billy's car seat in our hands.

A few hours later, at about 11am, a Buddhist nun appeared
in her yellow and red robe. It was comforting to see her,
although she was different from how I knew Buddhist monks
to be in Mongolia. She was a white woman in her 50s with a
shaved head. Her name was Susan. She was very gentle and
careful in her movements and warm in her manner. I wondered if she read her blessing in English. She said that she
did. That was a good thing to hear. In Mongolia, I was used
to hearing monks reading and praying in Tibetan. I didn't
know what exactly they were saying and I felt monks some-
how had this hidden mystique. When I was young, I would
follow my parents and grandparents, copying whatever they
did without any real understanding. Susan gave her blessing
to Billy, reading aloud some prayers; then she touched his
head with her prayer beads. I was grateful that we managed
to say goodbye to Billy in this way.

Jackie brought Sara and Simon to the hospital. Simon was
too young to understand what was going on and he just
wanted to have lunch in the canteen. So Jackie took him
out of the room. Sara was there looking worried, instinctively knowing it was serious. I spoke to her in Mongolian.
I said, 'Billy is not at all well. We are saying our goodbyes
now. Let's pray with the nun now.' Sara and I were praying with the nun, our hands clasped in prayer, our eyes
closed, whispering, '*Um ma ni badmi hum.*' I couldn't bring
myself to tell Sara that Billy was dying. It was hard. Sara
noticed that Billy was very blue, and she gave him her last
kiss. Richard was sitting behind us, feeling the same as me,

finding it hard to know how to break the news to Sara. The nun asked if I wanted her to be in the hospital for a while. I was grateful that she offered. I knew from experience that Buddhists have prayers to offer after someone has died. The Christian chaplain asked Richard if he wanted her to stay around. Richard didn't. So he thanked her and she left. The nun left us in the room to be on our own.

Billy's nurse that day was called Liz, a very professional and caring person. We were glad that we had her. We didn't want a nurse who lacked empathy and ignored us. We could tell that Liz was hurting for us.

Sara and Simon left with Jackie at about 1pm. It was a harrowing experience for them to be there for too long. Seeing their parents so fragile and their baby brother's last breaths in a scary hospital situation was too hard. Everyone was quiet. Richard, Jackie and I thought it was better if the kids were not there when we let Billy go. Jackie knows what it's like to lose someone. She had become a widow at 28 when she lost her first husband. My friend with her big heart had been through tough times herself.

After Sara, Simon and Jackie had left, Liz brought in some paints, paper, scissors and small plastic bags. At first I wasn't sure what she was going to do. Then I realised it was to take Billy's handprints and some of his hair. We wanted to do this when we made the decision to say our goodbyes to Billy. I chose green for the handprints. Our tiny boy's hands were dipped in some paint and put on clean sheets of white paper. Billy's hands and legs were weak now. I remembered being hurt by something a doctor had said to me after Billy was born. This young doctor came in and asked, 'Where is your baby? I heard your baby is floppy.' At the time, I felt like it was a freak show for them. She came to see my boy because he was floppy. Whatever had happened to non-judgemental and empathetic professionalism?

Liz and I took a lock from Billy's strawberry-blond hair. We couldn't believe his hair was red when he was born. He was the only one with red hair among all five of us. I joked with Richard, 'Don't look at me. Do your homework and see who had red hair in your family.' We soon found out that Richard's uncle Billy had had red hair when he was young. Uncle Billy is in his 90s now. So Billy shared not only his name but also his hair colour. We put the locks of Billy's hair in four little plastic bags for Richard, Sara, Simon and me.

I was phoning my parents every few minutes from the waiting room in the Intensive Care unit. They were in Uliastai, in their *ger*, thinking of us, with us in spirit. In the Mongolian tradition and horoscope, the date and time of someone's birth and death matter. I asked my parents which day it was better to let Billy go. It was then about 2.30pm in Britain and 10.30pm in Mongolia on Wednesday, 24th February 2010. My dad said, 'Wednesday.' That was fine because we had arranged with the consultant to turn off Billy's ventilator soon.

Richard and I knew we had to let Billy go soon. Our tiny little red-headed angel was still with us only because the machines were keeping him alive. It wasn't fair to him. We were keeping him alive for our sake. We loved Billy so much that we had to let him go. Liz brought in an armchair and covered it with a clean white sheet. Richard had a cuddle first, still with all the machines and monitors attached to Billy. It was his last cuddle while Billy was with us. Richard tilted his head down close to Billy and looked at him with a loving and gentle look in his face, treasuring the precious last moments. I could tell he was crying inside; his eyes were watery and he was having difficulty holding himself together, feeling fragile emotionally. I took their photo with my phone. These moments were never going to happen again. Then I took over from Richard, holding Billy as close as I could. I wanted him to die in our arms, on my lap, where he was born, where he was fed and where he was loved. We certainly didn't want him to die on an operating table, traumatised, and with strangers.

When we felt we should let Billy go, the doctors made him 'comfortable' by upping his morphine dosage. They turned the monitors away from us and left Billy with the ventilator and the pulse oximeter. Then the consultant asked if we were ready. We looked at each other and nodded together. The consultant quickly took out the ventilator and left the three of us alone in the room. Billy started to cry, gasping for breath and then he stopped breathing. Within thirty seconds Billy had gone. He had left us. He had left us forever. Richard and I held Billy's body, holding onto each other, our loud sobbing cries filling the room. For a while, I don't know how long, we cried and sobbed, covered with our tears of grief. Life wasn't fair. Billy was our baby. He was supposed to outlive us. We should have cut his hair for him to go to school, not for a keepsake. We were supposed to play with him, read him stories, hold his hand and walk along the streets, throw him in the air and give him hundreds and millions of kisses. I carried him for nine months dreaming of many things, but not to say goodbye and hold him like this, dead in my arms. We wouldn't even see his first smiles. We looked at Billy, who was now calm and pain-free.

After we had finally recovered our composure, Liz and the consultant came in. They checked Billy, and the consultant left us after having explained what would happen next. Liz told us that Meryl, our friend from Edinburgh, was outside. It was nice of Meryl to come, but she had just missed Billy. Meryl was the director of studies in the language school where I had done my course in London 10 years previously. She was the person who had replied to the email message that had changed my life. We had kept in touch and had become firm friends.

Meryl came in and spoke to us and kept us company. It was nice and comforting. Richard and I didn't have many relatives here. Richard's family are very few and old. His mother was now in a nursing home, not aware of how things were. My relatives were all in Mongolia, apart from one cousin in Germany. So having Meryl with us was touching. She left after a while, offering her help if we needed anything.

I cleaned Billy's face and body with Liz, as he was covered with bits of sticky tape that had been holding the tubes and needles in place. Billy looked perfect without the feeding tubes, catheter, needles and the ventilator. As soon as he was clean and ready I swaddled him in the blanket I had bought before he was born. I held Billy against me as tight as I could and let out a loud sobbing cry. That was the way I could imagine him to be, alive, with his mummy, held tight and loved. Richard and I took turns to hold Billy, our red-haired boy with Mongolian blue spots.

Three hours after Billy's last breath we left the hospital, at about 6.30pm. Richard's friend Alan came to give us a lift home. Liz took us to the hospital exit, shook Richard's hand and gave me a warm hug. We were so grateful for how she had treated us. She was professional, empathetic and caring. We thanked her and drove home. The world was crying with us. The sky was heavy with dark clouds. It was snowing and windy. The trees were covered with snow, which reminded me of Siberia. The road reminded me of Mongolian roads in the countryside, covered with snow;

following the tracks from the car in front was the only way to keep to the road.

Richard and I sat together holding hands in the rear seat of Alan's car. Alan and Richard had been friends since they were in primary school. Alan was a good friend and had been there for us over the years. Richard and I had to let people know about Billy. We sent text messages to our friends: 'Billy passed away peacefully in our arms at 3pm today.'

The text messages started to come in: 'I'm so sorry. There are no words that can describe what you are going through. Our thoughts are with you.' 'We feel for you. Will be in touch in due course.' 'My heart is broken for Billy and for you all. I know you must be suffering dreadfully. Please rest assured you are all in my heart, thoughts and prayers.' It was touching to receive them. We had people who cared for us and I felt like hugging them all and crying my heart out.

I gave Jackie a call to let her know that we were on our way. Poor Jackie had been there all day with the kids, feeding them and looking after them. Her own children were with her mother-in-law. She had had to hide her feelings about Billy until we got home. It must have been hard.

Alan dropped us home and drove to Glasgow. It was getting dark and the road was bad. He needed to go home himself, to his family. They had had a baby daughter a month before Billy.

As we came in, Sara and Jackie were waiting for us and Simon had fallen asleep. Sara was watching *Eastenders*. That gave us time to talk to Jackie, who was upset and trying hard to be strong for me and for all of us. Then I noticed that *Eastenders* had finished. Sara knew I was about to tell her something. She looked at me, scared. She looked as if she wanted to hide and didn't want to hear what I was about to say. I spoke to her in Mongolian. 'Billy is not coming home,' I said, sitting on my knees looking into Sara's eyes. She looked at me blankly. She asked, '*Billy nas barsan yum uu?*' – 'Billy died?' – I nodded. She went into a panic; she couldn't breathe properly, standing there and then slumping into the armchair. Her tears tumbled down her cheeks and she didn't want me to hug her at first. I comforted and talked to her and then she allowed me to hug her. It was hard. It was hard to see Sara going through this. She had been taking Billy's baby suit to bed with her since he'd been admitted to hospital. I couldn't. I wanted Billy, not his clothes. But now that's all I had left of him.

By now, Jackie had gone home and Sara went to bed. Richard and I sat for a while in the living room in our seats, staring and replaying scenes with Billy in our minds. Then we went to bed, shattered emotionally and physically. Jackie and Sara had changed our bedding. They had done anything they could to make us feel better. I couldn't remember the last time I had changed the beds, probably a month or so ago. We were too busy dealing with Billy's survival, leaving everything on hold, and concentrating on him. We had tried to keep things as normal as we could for Sara and Simon. That's why we had stayed at home and had let Sara go to school and Simon go to his nursery. There were times when Richard and I had just said hello in the hall and passed the car key to one another. One was going to the hospital and the other one was coming home from there.

The next day, as soon as we woke up, Richard started crying. We told Sara not to go to school. We pulled ourselves together and got ready to organise the funeral. Richard went to get the death certificate and I made phone calls to Mongolia. My mum wasn't well herself, after just getting home from Scotland. So my dad was coming back for the funeral alone. My uncles and aunts wanted to come, but it was too complicated with visas. Luckily my parents' visas were still valid for another couple of months.

On the 5th March 2010, Billy's funeral service took place in St Meddan's Church in town. We had Billy's coffin overnight at home. We put in photos of us, one of me breastfeeding Billy, and a canvas with Billy's other name – Sanchir. I'd written Sara and Simon's Mongolian names on canvas and put them in their rooms, so I wanted Billy to have his beside him, too. I gave him the name Sanchir when he died. It's not a convention, it was just my decision. *Sanchir* means Saturn. So that Billy will be bright in the sky among the stars. Also Billy was born on a Saturday. Sara made a *buuz* from clay for Billy, Richard wrote a letter, I put some money in a little Mongolian purse and Jackie and her family put in purple pom-poms. When he finally arrived, my dad brought some incense, nine miniature jewel stones and a Buddhist script to put inside the coffin. Richard and I had chosen a light-blue coffin with pictures of teddy bears holding balloons. I clothed Billy in a Mongolian brown silk *deel* that Simon had worn before, and put a top on saying, 'My sister loves me.' He also wore his Mongolian camel-wool shoes with silver bells on them.

The funeral service was fitting, with a Christian minister and the same Buddhist nun both saying their prayers. They all agreed that Billy was a symbol of union. He represented a joining of cultures, love, relationships and religions. I read the poem I had written for Billy in Mongolian. Everyone had a funeral service sheet, which Richard had made himself with the kids and my dad. He couldn't trust anyone else to do it. They had ribbons and little felt cars and trucks in different colours on them, each one unique. Simon and Sara had had different tasks. Sara had tied the ribbons and Simon had stuck the cars on. Richard had wanted the kids to be involved and to remember taking part. We dreamt of Billy playing at the sandy beach, building little sandcastles and sand *gers* with his big brother and sister, celebrating our birthdays together...

Epilogue

April 2010

Dear Billy,

I can't believe it's been seven weeks already since you passed away. It's been sunny lately and Mummy has thought about you a lot. Mummy dreamt of taking you out for a walk in your nice red pram, bringing you to the beach and letting you try ice-cream.

Your Scottish granny passed away exactly a month after you. So we had two funerals in four weeks. We miss her, too. Today we got up as normal and your daddy went to work. Mummy could tell he was down and very vulnerable emotionally. He went to work because, what else can we do? Your brother and sister are on holiday this week. It's the Easter break. They took an Easter egg and a bunny for you, to your grave. Yesterday, on the 49th day, we took you beautiful flowers and candles. You also have a solar lamp – it comes on when it's dark and the light looks like candle-light, with a warm colour like a flame. Altogether you have two lanterns, the solar lamp, a ceramic teddy and another teddy that Simon painted for you – it's holding a heart with writing on it. It says: 'We love you, Billy. Simon and Sara XXXXX.' Simon held that teddy bear himself on the train and in the car till he could put it on your grave. Your brother and sister also laid down some shells and pebbles, and your sister made a little *ger* for you too. You wouldn't know what a *ger* is: it's a round Mongolian house, made of felt and wood. Mummy grew up in one of those. They are very cosy and comfortable.

After taking flowers for you, Mummy gave some money to the ice-cream kiosk at the beach, so that they could give away ice-cream to children. We stayed there for a short time. People were happy with their 'free' ice-cream and waved at us, saying, 'Thank you.' The girl at the kiosk was telling people it was to remember you.

There was a mini-bus full of people. When they started coming off the bus, Mummy noticed that some of them had Down's syndrome. Mummy needs to be careful now. She finds herself staring at them, trying to picture how you would have looked and wanting to say 'Hello' to them. We miss you, baby. We are going to your grave now to light some candles. We love you, baby boy, Mummy's little boy. XXX

March 2011

Hallo Billy Buuz,

Today is Mother's day. We remember finding out that we were expecting you on Mother's day in 2009. The best present ever, Mummy and Daddy thought. Today it was a nice day. Your brother and sister made me a lovely card and as always they included your name when they signed it for Mummy. So thank you, Billy. Your brother was talking to Jackie yesterday. Jackie said, 'You will be a big brother.' He replied, 'Again.' He is right, you are going to have a baby sister soon.

Mummy also started writing a book in memory of you. She wanted to make you live in people's minds. She has written a short story in the *Scottish Family Legends* book called 'Fairytale Hero'. Your ginger hair with your Mongolian blue spots reminded Mummy of the fairytale heroes in Mongolia. Mummy was so pleased when The Scottish Book Trust let Mummy know that they would publish the story in the book. The book launch is in June at the BBC. Not long to go, but your baby sister is due around that time. Let's hope she will be born after the launch. Mummy's lovely babies. We love you all dearly. Night, Billy. XXXX

●

August 2012

Hallo Billy Buuz,

Your baby sister was one in June! The time flies. We called her Karen and she was born exactly one day after the book launch Mummy was telling you about! Remember, Mummy said she was writing a book? Well, that book won a trophy. That's for you, baby. Mummy had sent some sample chapters off to the Scottish Association of Writers' conference competition and hoped for a mention, never mind winning it. The book is called *Mongol*. There is a reason.

Mummy had a glimpse of how this term 'Mongol' can be used in different ways and with various meanings. Mummy thought to herself, perhaps Mummy is being oversensitive and touchy.

Then one day, a tweet startled Mummy when she was scrolling through the Twitter feed: 'Ricky Gervais, please stop using the word "mong".' It was October 2011. There were also articles about it in the *Guardian*, the *Daily Mail* and the *Telegraph*. Basically, a well-known British comedian called Ricky Gervais, whom Mummy and Daddy used to watch, had put up photos of himself making silly faces and retweeted 'Two mongs don't make a right...'

This comment sparked off memories of other incidents when Mummy had heard these terms – which are derived from the word 'Mongol' – being used negatively. One doctor's words came back to haunt Mummy: 'Billy's condition might not be so visible because of your background.'

Mummy and Daddy now know the background of this term only too well. Your diagnosis meant we read anything and everything to do with Down's syndrome. It was considered normal to use the term 'Mongol' from the 1860s to the 1960s throughout the world. A British doctor, John Langdon Down, who had discovered Down's syndrome in the 1860s, described it as 'Mongolism' and people as 'Mongoloid'. In his opinion, there were similar physical characteristics between people with Down's syndrome and people from Mongolia and the Mongoloid race.

Mummy has been raising awareness of this term through her writing in magazines and by speaking on radio locally in Scotland and on television in Mongolia. Since Mummy started raising awareness and talking about the term, she's come across many different attitudes. Mummy once met someone, for instance, who told her that Mongolians do look as if they have Down's syndrome. 'Yes, the flat face.' He relentlessly pressed on with his explanation. Mummy was upset, in tears.

Mummy hopes that one day the Mongolian ethnicity will not be confused with any genetic condition. And that people with disabilities and their loved ones won't have to hear this word being used as an insult. Good night, Billy. Mummy's beautiful baby boy. Love you. XXX

Recipe for buuz dumplings

I have never made *buuz* from a recipe. This is the first time I'm writing down the instructions that have been passed down the family. Traditionally, they are made with beef, mutton, lamb, goat meat, horse meat or sheep stomach. My mother sometimes used to mix some pre-cooked rice or chopped potatoes with the meat. In Scotland, we make them with turkey, which we've found is really tasty.

Dough

500g plain flour
1 tsp salt
250ml lukewarm water

1   Put the salt in the water and stir it until dissolved.
2   Sift the flour into a medium-sized bowl and make a well in the middle. Gradually pour in the water, drawing the flour towards the centre of the bowl with your fingers until you have formed an evenly mixed dough.
3   Knead the dough until smooth.
4   Place dough in a bowl, cover and leave it to rest for about 20 minutes.

Filling

400g minced beef
1 chopped onion
4 cloves garlic, finely minced
1 tsp salt
1 beef stock cube
50ml lukewarm water

1   In a large bowl, mix the beef, onion, garlic and salt.
2   Dissolve the stock cube in water and add to the mixture.

Making the buuz
1   Knead the dough again and roll it out thinly on a floured surface.
2   Cut the dough into circles about 8–10cm in diameter. We use the rim of a glass, but you can use pastry cutters.
3   Using a teaspoon, dot the filling in the centre of each circle, close them like parcels and crimp the edges with your fingers, making round or oval-shaped dumplings.

Cooking
Fill the steamer with boiling water and oil the steamer tray lightly.

1   Place the *buuz* in the steamer tray, ensuring they have sufficient space in between to avoid them sticking to each other – they will expand a little during steaming.
2   Steam for 15–20 minutes (larger dumplings will need more time than smaller ones) and keep the lid on until the time is up.
3   Carefully remove from the steamer and fan air over them for about 30 seconds. (This part is critical. My mum always highlighted that good buuz depend on this final touch).
4   Serve hot with ketchup, soy sauce, plum sauce or chilli sauce – or create your own variation.

Enjoy!

Footnote

In 1965 the World Health Organization (WHO) officially dropped references to 'mongolism'.

Acknowledgements

I want to thank my dear parents who shared their stories and have believed in me all my life. I love you both. I also want to thank my sister for her love and encouragement. I'm so sorry I'm on the other side of the world when you need me.

My thanks go to David Scott, the Honorary Consul of Mongolia in Scotland for his support and encouragement.

I would like to thank my friend Jackie, who is my babysitter, counsellor, driver and everything a friend can be. Thank you for helping me with the early drafts of this book. I am indebted to Freddie, who untangled my sentences and made sense and acted as a mentor for the whole process of this book. Thank you so much Freddie. I would like to thank Nick who also edited at the early stage. His comment 'It's like gold in many layers' kept me writing.

My thanks also go to Ayr Writers' Club, whose members welcomed me with open arms in time of need. I was delighted to win the Scottish Association of Writers award for a non-fiction book in 2012. My grateful thanks to the adjudicator for recognizing my book as a worthy winner in this category.

My sincere thanks to my editor Ali and my publisher Sara and everyone at Saraband for helping me achieve what I wanted, publishing this book.

More love and more thanks to many friends who supported this book, especially Karen, Simon, Susan, Ian and Eddy.

Finally, thanks to my wonderful husband who has stood by me through good times and bad times. You have no idea how much you mean to me.